Buying a Home

Also published by Virgin Books:

Dating: The Virgin Guide
Entertaining: The Virgin Guide
Money: The Virgin Guide

About the author

Ben West has written on a wide variety of subjects for many
newspapers and magazines including *The Guardian*, the
Independent, *The Daily Telegraph*, *The Times*, *The Daily Mail*, *The
Evening Standard* and *Readers' Digest*. He was chief property
correspondent of *The Daily Express* and *The Sunday Express* from
1999–2001. His other books include *London for Free*, *Fun for a
Fiver in London* and *Fun for a Fiver in Amsterdam*.

Buying a Home

The Virgin Guide

Ben West

First published in Great Britain in 2003 by
Virgin Books Ltd
Thames Wharf Studios
Rainville Road
London
W6 9HA

A catalogue record for this book is available from the British Library.

ISBN 0 7535 0773 0

Typeset by Phoenix Photosetting, Chatham, Kent
Printed and bound in Great Britain by Mackays of Chatham, Chatham, Kent

CONTENTS

INTRODUCTION

Property has long been a national obsession, but recently our love of bricks and mortar has reached gargantuan proportions.

In the last five years or so television programmes have emerged concerning all aspects of property and many of these have become some of Britain's most popular programmes. Newspapers have been devoting more and more pages to the subject, DIY is booming as never before, and the incredible upwards march of house prices in many areas has caused us to look for increasingly ingenious housing solutions.

In many regions, where property prices have rocketed, getting on to the property ladder can seem a daunting task. One of the intentions of this book is to show that there are many routes to owning a home, and many of these options are seldom considered.

Whether you are tentatively considering buying a home or are already installed in the property of your dreams and are looking to extend or let or move, this book will hopefully guide you effortlessly through the maze.

Note: Professional and trade associations and organisations mentioned in the text are listed with the address, telephone number and website address in the directory at the back of the book, while contact details for relevant companies are listed at the end of chapters throughout the book.

1 RENTING v BUYING

WHY BUY INSTEAD OF RENT?

Unless you are an eternal nomad and your desire to travel causes you to not stay in one place for much longer than it takes to boil a kettle, owning a home has clear advantages over renting.

For starters, over time you can benefit from having made a long-term investment rather than paying your monthly cheque for a landlord's benefit. The amount you make of course depends upon the type of property, its location and the timing of your purchase.

In many parts of the UK the rent is often more than the amount you would pay on a mortgage for a similar property. Overall, buying is cheaper than renting. In 2002, Abbey National Bank estimated that over 25 years, buying an average property in the UK would be £101,679, or 30 per cent cheaper than to rent one. The year before it said that it cost 57 per cent less to buy than rent, due to steep property price increases and a growth in buy-to-let properties causing slightly reduced rents.

Abbey National calculated the average rent on a two-bedroom flat in the UK to be £528 a month, which over 25 years and allowing for inflation of 4 per cent would cost a total of £263,785. Buying such a property, which had an average price of £73,583, would cost £426 a month in mortgage repayments based on interest charged at 6 per cent and a 10 per cent deposit. With maintenance costs included, buying the property would have saved £121,815 over 25 years, and the owner would also own the flat outright and have benefited from any increase in house prices.

The property market can change dramatically very quickly, so it is often dangerous to assume you can buy property in the short term and make a quick buck. As a rule of thumb, buying with the intention of staying put for at least ten years should see you through potential problems like a market crash and recovering from negative equity.

In many parts of our overcrowded land we have seen spectacular price rises in recent years, making it harder and harder to get on the property ladder. But, again, prospective buyers should be wary of buying any property simply to get on the ladder. In a downturn the least desirable properties swiftly become virtually unsaleable as the plunge in prices allows first-time buyers to sidestep them and afford better ones. The recession of the late 1980s saw many buyers saddled with virtually unsaleable studio flats, because most buyers preferred and could afford bigger properties.

Despite such potential pitfalls, there are a number of reasons why it can be very advantageous to buy rather than rent. The chief one is that you are getting no return on the money when you pay rent. Many tenants are at the mercy of their landlords, who may charge high rents, provide low-quality furniture, skimp on maintenance and provide their tenants with bad service.

Although there are notable exceptions all around the country, if you own a property it is likely to rise in value and if you later wanted to leave you have the choice of either selling up or retaining it and renting it out, in the process hopefully making a good profit. If you do sell and decide to rent, you attain first-time buyer status again and are not trapped in a chain, making it easier to buy again in the future.

Before buying remember that a property incurs substantial costs like estate agent's, solicitor's and surveyor's fees and stamp duty. Whatever the recent history, your property won't automatically go up in value. It may fall substantially – which could lead to negative equity (owing more on your mortgage than the property is worth) – as thousands of homeowners discovered in the early 1990s. Bear in mind that the monthly mortgage is only one cost of ownership – others include insurance, maintenance and repair. Also, by buying you're committing yourself to monthly payments – how secure are your job or career prospects?

Of course, renting has its advantages too. You don't have the long-term commitment, the ongoing maintenance and running expenses. Be informed, and you have loads of rights as a tenant. You are not tied down if you are uncertain of where you want to live or plan to move jobs. Renting also allows you to investigate an area before making a commitment.

It can be a good idea to rent temporarily if you have bought a property that needs a lot of work doing to it as the builders will be able to work more quickly and you can avoid a lot of disruption.

If you are selling in order to move, it can make sense to sell your home and rent until you buy, as long as you are not in a market where prices are rising quickly. Being a cash buyer means you are not at the mercy of a chain and being able to move fast means you are less likely to be beaten by someone coming in with a higher offer (gazumping). But bear in mind that you may have to pay to store your furniture and belongings and two moves are obviously costlier and more time consuming than one.

RENTING

If you are renting, find a property from an agent that is a member of a relevant professional organisation such as the Association of

Residential Letting Agents (A.R.L.A.), which imposes a code of practice on members.

In general, renting through a letting agency is for a minimum of six months, meaning that you have the option to stay for a year but also can give two months' notice any time after you have rented the property for four months.

The landlord should provide an *assured short-hold tenancy agreement,* typically lasting six or twelve months for both parties to sign. This gives the landlord a guaranteed right to repossess the property after the period of tenancy has expired.

A tenant has more rights instead agreeing to an *assured tenancy,* which provides the tenant with the right to stay at the property as long as the landlord cannot provide a valid reason to gain possession, such as substantial rent arrears. Go for this type of agreement if it is possible to, although a landlord may expect a higher rent because of the extra security you enjoy. It is a good idea to ask for a clause in the contract allowing you to quit the property for reasonable reasons such as a job relocation. Company, holiday and student lets, lettings by resident landlords and occupational lets such as a porter's flat in an apartment block are all not covered by these rules.

A rental agreement should at the very least contain the following conditions, which are so fundamental they are considered binding, whether included or not. They are that the landlord must keep in repair the structure and exterior of the property, as well as installations for supply of electricity, gas and water, and water heating and sanitation. If furnished accommodation is offered, the furniture must comply with fire and safety regulations. If the landlord neglects his responsibilities, a tenant can approach the local authority to take action via a magistrate and, if necessary, appeal to their MP.

The tenant is expected to pay the agreed rent, and any changes to the property require approval by the landlord. The tenant is entitled to live free of disturbance by the landlord, although the landlord can gain access to the property by giving 24 hours' written notice.

When looking for a rental property, have a month's rent (or enough for a quarter, if that is the terms of the agreement), and a deposit equivalent to a month's rent (or even six weeks) ready, and references from your current employer, bank and previous landlord will speed things up.

When you're searching for a property, don't be afraid to take your time viewing. Check you know what is included and whether there are additional costs. Ensure the main services are connected and working, and turn on the central heating and check the radiators are heating correctly. Try all working parts in the kitchen and bathroom, such as the cooker, washing machine, shower and taps.

Look carefully at any neighbours using your communal staircase. Ask the landlord or agent to show you certificates proving the safety of any gas installations.

The next stage is the drawing up of the tenancy agreement, which you should read carefully, however uninspired reading it may be. You may have to pay the fee to a credit reference agency if this has been used to ascertain whether the landlord or agency thinks you are a satisfactory tenant.

When you move in, the landlord or his agent should check you into the property, where you will sign documents relating to the furniture, equipment and condition of the property. You should point out anything they may have missed out, such as a damaged table or stained carpet, to avoid problems later. Meter readings should be taken at this time. Most landlords and agents expect the rent to be paid by standing order.

As a tenant you will normally be responsible for having the telephone reconnected and for paying council tax and the television licence. If you are sharing, you will all have 'joint and several' responsibility, meaning that if one tenant causes damage or does not pay the rent, all tenants are responsible. If you are a single occupier, you are entitled to a 25 per cent discount on the tax.

You will be responsible for the general maintenance and upkeep of the property, such as keeping water pipes from freezing up in winter, replacing light bulbs and replacing an appliance broken through misuse.

More serious problems, such as a central heating breakdown, should be attended to by the landlord or agents within 24 hours, but if the problem falls on a holiday or the boiler is out of action for a few days with reasonable excuse, such as awaiting a spare part, you cannot withhold rent.

If you feel the rent is too high, when the lease comes up for renewal contact your local council's Rent Assessment Officer.

EXTRA INFORMATION

There is a useful chapter on the legalities of letting and renting in *Law Without A Lawyer* by Fenton Bresler.
www.themovechannel.com has guides on rental agreements as well as lots of other subjects. The UK-wide
www.accommodationforstudents.com lists rooms in halls of residence, private rentals and housing schemes. **www.loot.com** has plenty of flatsharing opportunities. Shelter can provide various publications concerning renting.

2 GETTING READY TO BUY

STEPS TO A QUICK, EASY MOVE

HOW LONG DOES IT TAKE TO BUY A HOME?

The process of finding a home, from the initial house-hunting to completing the purchase, currently takes an average of around six months.

This breaks down into an average of twelve weeks or so from beginning to look for a home to having your offer accepted; another four weeks or so from acceptance of the offer to having a mortgage offer; another four weeks from receiving the mortgage offer to exchange of contracts; and a further two weeks from exchange of contracts to completion.

Those with experience of buying a home may question these figures, especially if they have seen a sale fall through or a chain collapse. Indeed, around a third of accepted offers fail to reach completion.

QUICKENING THE BUYING PROCESS

With so many things to consider, and so many factors that need to fall into place, buying a new home can be an incredibly stressful business. Do the building's timbers harbour more bugs than London Zoo's insect house? Is the property only marginally better an investment than an ice cream factory in the Arctic? Do your children have as much chance getting into the only decent school nearby as you do winning the Lotto jackpot? Will your party-mad neighbours be recreating an Ibiza nightclub each Saturday just as you're ready for a kip?

Added to the stresses, many buyers omit to do the homework that can save buckets of time and money and instead go about house buying as if they were buying a pair of shoes. They'll walk along the high street and pop into the estate agents, taking the agent's advice as gospel even though he is paid by and represents the seller. It's a ludicrous situation. In America you often have a buyers' agent representing you. Nobody would go into the stock market and spend their life savings without asking the advice of an expert. Is there any other market in the world where everything's geared to help the seller and not the buyer?

Fortunately, there are many ways of making things work to your advantage, and the modern house-hunting process can be easily speeded up, allowing even the most overloaded workaholic a chance to buy their dream home.

But before you can talk about wanting a study or a south facing garden you've got to know that you can afford property in the area you want.

Your first port of call should be to lenders to see how much you can borrow. Lenders can provide a certificate indicating that you have a mortgage agreed in principle, and this shows you are serious when you put in an offer on a property.

If you have a property to sell your first contact with estate agents should not be to see what properties are available, but to ask them to value your existing one. Valuations can vary widely, so ask at least three or four agents to get a good idea of your current property's worth. Trying to sell your existing property before you begin your search can speed things up as you're ready to move in, which is far more attractive to a seller than a buyer waiting to sell his existing home.

It is crucial for a buyer strapped for time to be well prepared before beginning the search. Spending a bit of time at the outset deciding upon the location and finding an efficient solicitor can save many frustrated hours later on. If you've invested many hours only to see the sale collapse because you can't arrange a mortgage in time is doubly frustrating if you didn't really have the time to spare anyway.

Write down everything that you want and try and put your requirements in an order of importance. Space, price and location are the key things.

Rather than spending an age on the high street you can sort out many things in far less time on the telephone or Internet, including arranging a mortgage and insurance, property searching and getting on estate agents' mailing lists.

Survey the local market to work out the type of property you can afford, walk the neighbourhood to ascertain what the shops and services are like and the furthest you'd be happy to travel to the nearest station. If you have children, would you be happy with the local schools, and would you be in the catchment area? Ask the local police station what the crime rates are like. Take a drive to see how easy it is to park. Once you've done homework like this and are able to focus on a specific area you could and would want to live in, you won't be wasting time investigating tempting properties in areas you'd never want to move to.

If you've no time, consider buying a newly built home. Not only are you not threatened by a chain, but an increasing number of housebuilders offer a bespoke service so that you can swiftly order tiles, carpets, paint and worktop finishes, lighting arrangements, power point positions and the endless other choices in a brainstorming couple of hours as if you were shopping at the supermarket.

When looking for a home, take someone with you so that you get a second opinion before you put in an offer. They may pick up potential problems or drawbacks you miss in your enthusiasm. View at different times of day as the property may be far noisier at rush hour, or when the nearby restaurant opens.

Follow your gut feeling. It is often said that a buyer 'just knows' when they have found the right property. Wait for that moment rather than rushing into buying something just because you are tired of searching.

Accept that an accepted offer doesn't guarantee the property. Before the vendor is legally bound to sell to you be prepared for someone to put in a higher offer, or for the housing chain you're in to collapse and scupper your plans.

When the conveyancing (legal) process kicks in, it is worth paying for a personal local authority search to speed things along. Searches, which check that there are no forthcoming potential problems like a development that could adversely affect your property, typically take about two weeks but by paying a bit extra you can have a personal search, cutting the wait to just two or three days.

You can also reduce the period between exchange and completion. There are usually a few weeks between exchange and completion, but as long as other parties in the sale have no objections, legally you can complete sooner, even on the same day.

3 WHEN, WHERE AND WHAT TO BUY

WHEN TO BUY

The property market strengthens and weakens considerably at different times of year and if you ignore the peaks and troughs you could miss out on the best times to buy, and find yourself as a buyer facing prices rising by the day.

Timing your buy is always a gamble, yet without the benefit of hindsight all you can do is try and anticipate trends and act upon them.

Traditionally, the market has usually picked up strongly in the spring, with prices and sales rising dramatically, only to tail off in the autumn. There tends to be an influx of enquiries in the new year, as people have decided to move in the coming year, but it doesn't tend to translate into sales until later.

Contrary to popular belief, on bank holidays and during all school holidays, including half terms, agents tend to see a clear drop in activity rather than busier times as people increasingly protect their precious leisure time. This can translate into some prices dropping as properties fail to budge.

Not only does the bad weather of winter discourage many buyers from searching for a home, but it puts off vendors too. They know that their home is likely to be looking increasingly less attractive than in the spring and summer, and will decide to wait until peak property market periods when they'll be more confident of a quick sale at a higher price. Things are quietest in December, as both buyers and sellers turn their attentions and budgets to Christmas.

There are too many factors involved to give a definitive answer, but possibly one of the best times to buy is when everyone else isn't. When there are few purchasers around you are not rushed into a decision and have far more bargaining power. In midsummer when the spring rush has subsided and the rest of the population is on holiday, there are invariably going to be sellers willing to be flexible and negotiate on price. Likewise, not only will vendors be especially keen to sell in the depths of winter, but you can see whether the home is working efficiently and is warm and weatherproof.

But ultimately the property market is so complex and influenced by so many factors that it is impossible to say definitively when is a good time to buy. If you decide to buy when prices are rising ferociously, you may be buying at the top of the market only to see prices fall and throw you into negative equity. Equally, if you decide to wait in the hope that prices may fall, they may instead continue to rise at a fast rate, making buying increasingly unaffordable.

The widening gulf between house prices and earnings has been causing many potential first-time buyers to be priced out of the property market for longer than in the past.

The good news is that at the time of going to press there has been a lengthy period where the cost of borrowing is very low. There are many more mortgage options than even just five years ago, and it is far easier to obtain a mortgage fixing you to a low interest rate for a lengthy period.

WHERE TO BUY

CITY v COUNTRY   Most city dwellers, especially if they have children, at some point consider leaving the urban big smoke for some rural tranquility. It's no surprise, with 60 per cent of the population stuffed into six per cent of the UK.

The natural beauty of the countryside is invigorating, and you usually get far more home and land for your money and insurance rates tend to be lower.

But beware of the cons. You are far more reliant on a car in the country, although driving is less of a problem with few traffic jams and less parking headaches.

For many people the reduced employment opportunities outside the cities can result in hidden extras like a hefty train season ticket and other transport costs. For example, an annual ticket from Norwich to London is currently nearly £5,000. Such costs can cancel out any savings made on the smaller mortgage or lower risk house contents and car insurance premiums those in rural areas usually enjoy.

Maintenance and domestic fuel costs usually increase in country homes. A small, terraced town house sheltered in a built-up area is more likely to be far cheaper to light, heat and maintain than a lone, large building on a secluded hill.

There are other factors to consider before taking the plunge into the rural lifestyle. For example, does the property have mains drainage? Could local farming cause disruption? Those used to the high density of population in a hectic big town may feel isolated living down a lonely country lane.

Many country areas become inhospitable in winter, because of fog, cold and snow. Doctors, hospitals, chemists and schools may be a significant distance away and local shops non-existent or badly stocked.

Socially there can be a lack of choice in the country and often it can take time to become accepted in a community. Yet the slower pace of living can encourage contact with neighbours and a generally friendlier atmosphere.

Pollution comes in different guises in the country – from chemical sprays used in farming, from spending more time in the car because the school run is thirty miles instead of three, from ozone, which is most prevalent in the countryside. Think twice if the dream cottage you wish to buy is near a coal-fired power station, as these emit about 70 per cent of the UK's sulphur dioxide and cause respiratory problems. Asthma sufferers should seek medical advice before moving from the city in an attempt to improve their condition: the disease can worsen in many rural areas due to the different triggers there.

And there's noise pollution. Some confirmed townies, used to next door's ghetto blaster pounding away on a Saturday afternoon, can't abide an inconsiderate cockerel crowing at some godforsaken hour. Prospective country buyers should also ask whether there is an airport or air force base nearby. The grounds of that idyllic pile, peaceful when you viewed it, won't be so attractive if it emerges it's near Britain's fastest growing airport and flight paths to the world's four corners.

The city generally offers more housing choices, more public transport, recreation, entertainment and shopping facilities, health care and schools, although housing is more likely to be costlier, health care overstretched and schools suffering from discipline problems. There may be less privacy, more noise and pressure in the city.

The secret to a successful move out of the city is not to attempt too much too soon. Going from a maze of busy streets to the back of beyond can be a costly, time-consuming mistake. It may be safer to consider moving to the edge of suburbia, where you have both rural peace and urban facilities nearby. Or letting your city home and renting in the country for a year to see whether it really is for you.

UP-AND-COMING AREAS Spotting the next up-and-coming area can still be highly lucrative. It can also be risky. Time it wrong and you could be buying after the price hikes. Or the prices might never grow to match the anticipation.

To successfully spot the next trendy area you often have to anticipate the knock-on effect of the last one. Employment and industry are important factors when making predictions on the property market. Areas with new incoming industry are places to watch. Areas suitable for the 'second home' market or of outstanding natural beauty can boost an area too.

Property prices can vary hugely in a small locality. Even seasoned city dwellers are often staggered by the extent by which property prices can differ, even in the same street. In some parts of London, houses side by side can vary by hundreds of thousands of pounds. But it's not just London. Penthouses costing £2 million are increasingly common in Manchester, for example, yet just a few miles away, at the time of writing, terraced houses in Salford have been for sale for as little as £1,000.

The centres of cities like Newcastle, Sheffield, Liverpool, Bristol, Cardiff and Birmingham have all enjoyed recent multi-million pound regeneration schemes with luxury loft apartments and flash penthouses being snapped up at unprecedented prices, yet nearby remain boarded up and vandalised run-down terraced homes going for as little as the price of a second-hand car.

Yet it's not just the cities that are split mercilessly between the haves and have-nots. Rural areas suffer from exactly the same divisions. For every healthily appreciating rural des res there's a low-rent eyesore in a property blackspot that won't shift even if almost given away.

Key drivers for higher house prices in rural areas are school performance, employment, the extent of amenities, crime levels and the road network. There are natural issues like the danger of subsidence, windstorm damage and flooding.

Even homes in pricey pockets can swiftly experience a change of fortune. A new retail park, traffic scheme or expanding airport can turn a property hotspot to cold overnight.

WHAT TO BUY

Before you start your search, work out in your mind exactly what you are looking for. Many prospective buyers waste untold time and money or experience disappointment because their search is too vague or in too large an area or buy on impulse because they have not thought through the consequences properly.

Before you even glance at an estate agent's window draw up a checklist of requirements. You could start with a wish list of things that would make your home ideal.

The list could include things like:

- **Georgian or Victorian**
- **at least three bedrooms**
- **a garage**
- **a large garden that enjoys the evening sun**
- **a quiet residential street very near a train station and shops**

Because few people have the budget to buy their ideal home you could translate the list above into a checklist of absolute minimum requirements.

This list could maybe include:

- **anything built before 1940**
- **two bedrooms plus lots of storage space**
- **off-street parking**
- **a small garden or large communal gardens, a roof terrace or balcony, or a park within walking distance**
- **public transport near enough to ensure good shopping facilities are less than ten minutes away and work less than forty minutes away**

There's often lots to weigh up. Although prices tend to drop the further you are from the town or city centre, travel times and costs may be substantially higher. If you have children will you be in the catchment area for a suitable school?

Don't let a property's charm cause you to disregard any practical advantages. A chocolate-box exterior is all very well but if the location of the property adds an extra thirty minutes to your journey to work the beautiful view may not be worth it.

CHECKLIST

Dream home
Location
City
Suburbs
Rural
Public transport nearby
Parking
Distance from shops
Distance from work
Within school catchment area

Property
House
Flat
Newly built home
Old property
Number of reception rooms
Large or small kitchen
Dining room

Study
Number of bedrooms
Number of bathrooms
Garden
Garage

Acceptable property

Location
City
Suburbs
Rural
Public transport nearby
Parking
Distance from shops
Distance from work
Within school catchment area

Property
House
Flat
Newly built home
Old property
Number of reception rooms
Large or small kitchen
Dining room
Study
Number of bedrooms
Number of bathrooms
Garden
Garage

4 TYPES OF HOUSING

HOUSING TYPES

Which is better: buying a wreck that looks like a bargain but – with the endless remedial work you unearth – may be a speedy way to the bankruptcy courts, or opting for an immaculate new-build home you can move straight into but which may be grossly overpriced?

HOUSING LAYOUTS

The advantages of buying a **basement flat** include the probability of having your own garden or at least a patio, and the possibility of your own front door. Disadvantages include less light, a greater likelihood of problems with damp and a greater security risk.

Open-plan homes appeal to those who like space and encourage very sociable living, with features like big reception areas or a kitchen/diner/living area. Yet such homes provide less personal privacy than more traditional configurations, can be costlier to heat and insulate, and more difficult to hide clutter from.

Terraced homes tend to be significantly cheaper than semi-detached and detached alternatives but off-street car parking and garaging is seldom an option and it can be especially problematic if you have noisy neighbours.

You are certainly less boxed in in a **semi-detached property** than in a terraced home but a noisy neighbour can still be a problem. Side access to the property increases the security risk slightly.

A **detached home** is many people's ideal, with neighbours at least a small distance away. Yet increased ease of access means less security than in a terraced or semi-detached house and as there is no party wall with neighbouring properties, there is an increased loss of heat and therefore higher heating bills a likelihood.

HOUSING TYPES

In order of price, very loosely starting with the most expensive, here are a number of the main housing types:

GEORGIAN

For many, the elegant and attractive classical proportions of a good example of the Georgian country or town house clad in white stucco, stone or brick, make this the ultimate property purchase. The sense of history, period features (like ironwork balconies, sash windows, attractive pediments, columns and fan lights) and pleasing architecture combine to make a lovely home destined to appreciate well, although maintaining such an old property can be both expensive and demanding.

LOFT AND PENTHOUSE APARTMENTS

Britain's inner cities have been overrun by this housing type in the 1990s. Typically converted from redundant industrial and commercial buildings, they are often located in up-and-coming quarters of a city, such as a riverside. Often double-height, open-plan and sleekly designed, they can look fabulous but can be very pricey, and costly to heat.

THE EXECUTIVE HOUSE

Ultra-modern inside but often a pastiche Georgian or Victorian affair outside, these invariably expensive homes, most often assembled in small cul-de-sac groupings upon prime greenfield land, are eternally popular with the upwardly-mobile type. Extras like en suite bathrooms attached to all bedrooms and double or triple garages abound.

VICTORIAN

Most residents of Victorian houses would rather be installed in something Georgian but as there aren't enough to go round the Victorian house is difficult to beat. Built in huge swathes across our cities and towns during a phenomenal period of urban growth, the Victorian house design, with its high ceilings and good-sized rooms, endures well, combining excellent aesthetics, density and layout. Most have cellars, a boon for storage.

EDWARDIAN

Less popular and distinguished than earlier house types, these comfortable homes nevertheless often feature things like tiling, panelling and stained glass.

THE 1930s SEMI

Dismissed as drearily suburban by many, this style, characterised by semi-circular bay windows and a red brick arch over the porch, spread up and down the new trunk roads like wildfire and usually has spacious rooms and a surprisingly large garden. You also tend to get a lot of space for your money.

MANSION FLAT

Common in the West End of London and other big cities and mainly built from around 1880 to 1910, these typically neo-Georgian buildings can be a bit dreary, house a maze of corridors and be located on a main road, but often boast a great address. They often have well-proportioned rooms with high ceilings but kitchens and bathrooms are often pokey and dated. They range from the badly maintained to luxurious.

PURPOSE-BUILT BLOCK

Apartments in purpose-built blocks, which have typically been built after the 1950s, plus many built during the 1930s, tend to be specifically designed for the purpose and are usually cheaper – and less imposing – than properties within grander mansion blocks. They may have low ceilings and thin walls.

CONVERSION FLAT

Conversions, which form part of a previous single-occupancy large house, often have interesting, big rooms, frequently with period features, but partition walls may be thin and therefore noise from other flats can be a problem. The common parts of the building, such as the hall and stairs, may be badly maintained.

BUNGALOW

Compact and ideal if you can't do with stairs, critics cite their tendency towards ugliness and inefficient use of land. Devotees speak of their flexibility – you can have a study rather than a second bedroom. They also often afford a good degree of privacy and tend to be good value because they are frequently considered unfashionable. For families there is no need for stair gates or a playroom as the children's bedrooms are on the same level.

EX-LOCAL AUTHORITY BLOCK

The right-to-buy scheme, introduced in 1980 and intended to 'empower' council tenants by allowing them to buy their homes at a significant discount, has caused over 1.5 million former council properties to come into the privately owned sector and while such properties used to usually be the cheapest of all, prices are gradually climbing. As the freeholder to such homes tends to be the local authority, service and maintenance charges tend to be comparatively cheap.

Such properties tend to be well designed with – as long as the location is good – clean but basic communal areas and good-sized living areas, and if you buy in a tower block, the views can be fabulous.

PARK HOMES

Unless you opt for the best, park homes are an inexpensive housing option. Sites can hold as few as five or six homes or as many as several hundred, and the homes cost from around £12,000 second-hand and from about £25,000 to over £100,000 new.

Being detached factory-built, timber-framed units, the homes boast particularly low running costs and require little maintenance. Park home sites are often geared to a specific niche market, and can be for holiday or residential use, or maybe for over-fifties only, or having attractions ideal for families. Pets are permitted at some parks while not at others.

When considering buying a park home, it is important to ascertain extra costs such as the site rent, which currently typically ranges from about £60 to over £100 per month, depending upon the area of the country and facilities in the park. Household costs like electricity and gas typically cost under £15 per week.

Questions to ask include whether the park is a member of the National Park Homes Council or the British Holiday and Home Parks Association. Each of these organisations enforces codes of practice.

It is prudent to ask by how much the pitch fee has increased in the last few years, and if there are age restrictions. Park conditions such as spacing between homes and the condition of park roads should comply with the local authority's site licence, which should be on display at the park.

Note that if the park does not have planning permission as a permanent residential park and you are required to vacate your home for several weeks each year, protection given by the 1983 Mobile Homes Act does not apply.

Such homes can also be sited singly in certain circumstances. Local authorities may give planning permission for park homes to be sited on freehold plots, or for their use as additional accommodation, such as a granny annex, in the garden of a traditional home.

Further information can be obtained from the National Park Homes Council and the British Holiday and Home Parks

Association. Monthly magazine *Park Home and Caravan* has details of many parks and park homes.

BUYING OLD

Many old properties ooze character and it is a misconception that they are far more difficult to maintain than newly built homes. Many older properties were built to very high standards using superior materials and boast thick, solid walls that today's homes can only dream of, and although building regulations are stricter than ever, many building practices and choices of materials used are made in the interests of saving money for the housebuilder rather than to create long-lasting, maintenance-free homes.

THATCHED HOMES

Most people would agree that thatched country cottages can be the ultimate in picture-postcard beauty. Yet they are also seen by many as a substantial fire hazard requiring regular costly maintenance.

There are, fortunately, a number of myths concerning thatched homes. For example, if you go to a specialist insurer, a thatched home need not be much more expensive to insure than a conventional home.

Because thatched homes are well insulated, you save on heating costs in the winter and they are also cool in the summer. Modern fire-retardant materials and new developments like fire-resistant barriers under the thatch have greatly reduced fire risks and make borrowing from building societies easier.

About 90 per cent of fire claims from thatched properties are chimney related and simple measures like having chimneys swept regularly, checking wiring and having a thatcher inspect the roof every five years can substantially reduce fire risk. You can also install a fire prevention system.

Although thatched homes require a bit more care and expense than the average home, the pros easily outweigh the cons. Because they're highly desirable they usually appreciate well.

New thatched roofs cost from around £10,000 for a small cottage and last from anything between a few years and over a century depending on the materials used. Before buying a thatched home, you can have the property inspected by a thatcher to establish the age and condition of the thatch, at a cost of around £200.

There are three main types of thatch: water reed, found in Norfolk, brittle, and lasting 50–60 years; combed straw (also misleadingly known as combed wheat reed), which is found in

Devon and lasts 25–40 years; and long straw, which is found all over the UK but least resilient and lasting 15–30 years. There have been some dramatic exceptions to these average lifespans. The ridge of the thatch will require replacing more regularly and costs about a third of the full job.

Council regulations and whether the building is listed may cause the local authority to insist on a certain material being used when re-thatching. Certain materials, like hard-to-find long straw, can increase costs considerably.

The Thatching Advisory Service provides a helpline, 24-hour emergency service and an annual survey for thatched home owners. The National Society of Master Thatchers can provide details of local thatchers.

LISTED BUILDINGS

Over half a million properties in the UK are listed, because of their architectural or historical interest or quality of design. The most important buildings or structures are listed Grade I or Grade II* and nothing can be done to change the structure, repairs must strictly be in keeping with the building and extensions are not permitted. The commonest listing is Grade II and changes require consent but there are fewer restrictions.

Listed buildings can sometimes qualify for grants for repairs, from bodies such as English Heritage or local authorities. Additionally, VAT is zero-rated for repairs to protected buildings.

Further information is available from SAVE Britain's Heritage, the Society for the Protection of Ancient Buildings and in Scotland the Scottish Civic Trust.

PROPERTIES WITH PLAQUES

Proud owners of one of the seven hundred prestigious properties included in English Heritage's popular Blue Plaque scheme, which identifies buildings that used to be the homes of famous residents as varied as Jane Austen, Oscar Wilde and Jimi Hendrix, may be in for a surprise. According to agents selling such properties, plaque status does nothing to increase the value of your property. It makes no difference to the price whatsoever, especially in this market where there's so much interest in decent property anyway. It's the last thing on people's minds.

Although a pretty Blue Plaque outside your home may do little to raise its value, the scheme is more popular than ever and English Heritage has extended the scheme to other cities, like Southampton, Portsmouth and Birmingham.

Numerous other organisations also put up plaques to commemorate famous ex-residents around the country.

RESTORATION AND REFURBISHMENT

Each year scores of worthwhile properties are allowed to fall into ruinous disrepair in this country. Fortunately, doing your bit to help save the UK's heritage, by buying and doing up a dilapidated property, can also net you great savings and big profits when you come to sell as the cost of buying a wreck and doing it up can be far less than buying an equivalent-sized property in top condition.

But such a project is not for the faint-hearted and you need buckets of patience and commitment. With so many things that could go wrong during the scheme – unforeseen extra building works, building regulation and planning hold-ups, raising finance, for instance – you could also have a major restoration drama on your hands, as Cary Grant found out so vividly in his 1930s classic film, *Mr Blandings Builds His Dream House*, and more recently Tom Hanks in *The Money Pit*.

One of the biggest difficulties when restoring and renovating is working out your budget. Few people take the time and effort to prepare detailed costings, and as a result prices can increase rapidly and alarmingly once the work begins. Many properties for renovation can harbour lots of unforeseen problems.

Ideally you should obtain plenty of professional advice, from experts like a surveyor, an architect and a builder with experience of similar projects. Don't underestimate how long the process takes. Planning permission and building regulation hold-ups are common.

One of the biggest obstacles is finding and securing a suitable property in the first place, as even the most ruinous tip can inspire immense interest from an army of prospective buyers.

Apart from regularly contacting agents, scouring property Internet sites and home renovation magazines, there are several organisations that provide details of properties with tiny price tags in need of restoration. SAVE Britain's Heritage is one, and annually brings out a report listing many endangered historic buildings of all types, ages and styles. It also publishes a number of publications about the subject.

The Scottish Civic Trust's register of buildings at risk throughout Scotland is growing at an alarming rate and now runs to around 2,000 buildings. Its annual bulletin has a wealth of buildings ranging from unlisted crofts to A-listed mansions in desperate need of renovation.

The Society for the Protection of Ancient Buildings (S.P.A.B.) is Britain's largest, oldest and most technically expert pressure group fighting to save old buildings from decay, demolition and damage. It regularly hears of the needless destruction of beautiful properties.

When you find a suitable property ask yourself whether it is right for you. A little dark cottage with low ceilings and small windows can't be transformed into an oasis of light without wrecking it, and a high-ceilinged barn won't be cosy and snug.

Read up about the building techniques and decorative styles that would be appropriate. S.P.A.B., for example, has various publications and courses.

Rather than gutting the building, you want to preserve the building's quirks that give it character, such as oddly shaped doors and bulging walls. Use traditional building techniques and materials: repointing with cement mortar, for example, may not allow the walls to breathe. Old buildings often do not suit damp-proof courses, which could cause moisture to move to previously dry parts. Likewise, masonry paint can lock moisture into walls. Investigate the possibility of receiving a grant towards the work.

Restoration may need planning permission so check with the planners at the local council, and if the property is listed you will require listed building consent to restore it. You will need to discuss your proposals with the conservation officer at your local council. Repairs to a listed building attract VAT at 17.5 per cent, although conversion is zero-rated. Take care to satisfy yourself that the work done to date has been legal as unauthorised work carried out to a listed building by one owner becomes the responsibility of the new owner when the building changes hands.

A full survey is invaluable and although it may list many potential defects, these are unlikely to all require attention immediately.

Raising finance to buy and do up a property in great need of repair can be more difficult than for a conventional home and high street lenders may not be able to help. The Ecology Building Society is a source that specialises in providing mortgages for homes in need of renovation. As well as having the deposit for the property, buyers are often expected to have at least 15 per cent of the valuation price available to spend on the first stage of work for a lender to take them seriously.

The work may require the services of professionals like an architect or builder. If so, use ones experienced in conservation work, who may take time to locate and may charge more. View previous work they have done to see whether you approve of their style. You should try to keep in regular contact with the builders during the work to avoid mistakes, which could be costly and time-consuming.

Don't be seduced by a low asking price for a property. Restoration costs regularly exceed the market price for the property had it been restored. Installing services like electricity and water to rural properties can be very costly indeed.

There are a number of organisations that can be approached in the search for interesting redundant properties. Education authorities may have details of redundant schools and schoolhouses. Brewery chains have estate managers who may be organising the disposal of redundant pubs and these often turn up at auction.

To find out the owner of redundant commercial property such as a warehouse, contact the local authority, which can provide the contact details of who pays the rates on the property. The British Rail Property Board can provide the names of their regional managers who deal with disused railway property. The Forestry Commission sells property in its forests, and its head office can provide a list of properties. For a church building, such as a church or rectory, contact the Redundant Churches Division of The Church Commissioners or the local diocesan office or registry.

Homebuilding and Renovating magazine, £2.75 monthly, features lots of tips and advice about renovating. Visit their website at **www.homebuilding.co.uk**. *House and Cottage Restoration* by Hugh Lander is an excellently written, informative book about the subject. S.P.A.B. publishes a helpful leaflet, *Look Before You Leap: guidelines to restoring an old building*, which is reproduced on its website.

Organisations that can help with advice on either sourcing or restoring buildings include the Ancient Monuments Society, the Society for the Protection of Ancient Buildings (S.P.A.B.), the Scottish Civic Trust, the Ulster Architectural Heritage Society, SAVE Britain's Heritage, the English Historic Towns Forum, the Georgian Group, the National Monuments Record Centre, the National Trust, the Royal Commission on Ancient and Historic Monuments of Wales, the Twentieth Century Society, the Vernacular Architecture Group and the Victorian Society.

Contact the British Wood Preserving and Damp-proofing Association for advice about tackling damp and wood preservation. If you have a traditional dry stone wall to restore, contact the Dry Stone Walling Association of Great Britain.

Organisations that give restoration grants include the Architectural Heritage Fund, Cadw (Welsh Historic Monuments), English Heritage, the Heritage Lottery Fund and National Heritage Memorial Fund, and the Historic Houses Association.

BUYING NEW

Buying a brand new home can sidestep many of the usual stresses of homebuying. For example, you avoid the uncertainties, costs and considerable time of buying a house in a 'sale chain' (although some buyers inevitably experience postponed completion dates and other problems), you avoid an estate agent's fee entering the equation, you don't have to worry about rotting timbers and rising damp and you may be able to take advantage of special offers, such as those specifically for first-time buyers.

As well as being shiny, new and clean, new homes conform to the latest building standards and advancements, which could include sophisticated security systems and the latest high-tech computer, heating, lighting and audio/visual systems. There may be carpeting, bathroom fittings, a fitted kitchen, new appliances and energy efficient features.

The downside is that you tend to get considerably less space for your money and many new properties lack character. Capital growth – the money you make on the property since the time you bought it – can be more difficult to achieve than for older properties.

It is important to choose your housebuilder carefully. Recent surveys by Zurich Insurance have found that two out of five buyers would not recommend their builder to a friend, at least half needed work doing to their homes in the year after moving in and fewer than a third said that their builder had attended to all their reported problems before moving in.

Newly built homes, except those built by the smallest developers, are usually covered by a recognised warranty such as that operated by the National House Building Council (N.H.B.C.), Zurich Insurance or Premier Guarantee. Such warranties typically ensure that if the developer goes bust before your home has been built, you will either get your deposit back or the property will be completed. Any fault occuring after the property has been built should be rectified but the schemes vary considerably and do not cover all problems.

It is important to buy a new home covered by such a scheme, especially as few lending institutions grant a mortgage on a new property without one or under the supervision of a suitably insured architect or surveyor.

Before buying, take a close look at the site. Is it tidy and well-managed? Small developments often grow into larger estates. If the development is next to open ground, check whether it has been earmarked for a later phase of building.

Ask the sales people lots of questions. What are the total number of houses planned for the development? Who looks after communal areas? How long will the construction work for the whole site take?

Bear in mind that the show home will have been designed very carefully and may be decorated to an unusually high standard with furniture chosen to enhance the rooms. There may be subtle extra lighting to make the property look bright and smaller-than-average furniture to make the rooms look bigger. The internal doors may be missing to further detract from the feeling of clutter.

When you have paid the reservation fee for a property is the time to fix up a mortgage and solicitor. Before completion, your solicitor should ensure that the final warranty scheme certificate has been received.

When the property is supposedly finished, have a good look around to see that the standard of work is acceptable before paying out. For example, has everything that was in the original specification been included? Has the whole of the interior been painted well? Unless any unacceptable or outstanding items are of a minor nature, where you should get a written undertaking that they will be sorted out, you should not complete until the matter is rectified.

The bank or building society may not advance the funds for the property until it is completed to its satisfaction and so there may be a tense period where the house is basically completed but cannot be occupied. If you have had to complete on your old home before being able to move into your new one, you may have to arrange temporary accommodation in the interim.

Newly built homes should be virtually maintenance free for several years, especially as today there are so many checks and strict building regulations to comply with.

With a new home you are unlikely to suffer problems that plague older properties like leaking roofs, widespread damp and subsidence. Yet new homes can have problems too, and, although generally far less necessary than for older homes, it can be a good idea to have a homebuyer's report (rather than a full structural survey) done before you move in.

New homes are newly decorated and usually come complete with many extras like carpets, curtains, a fitted bathroom and kitchen and appliances, which can be paid for gradually over the mortgage term. Because building regulations and insulation standards are now so strict, new houses are considerably cheaper to run than their older counterparts. A modern home can be as much as four times more energy efficient than its Victorian equivalent.

When you buy a new home, many developers, especially when sales are sluggish, will throw in a whole range of enticements, such as carpeting, white goods, payment of the deposit as well as legal fees, stamp duty, free garden landscaping, a TV/stereo package and cashbacks.

You may be able to make design and cosmetic changes before moving into a new home. The plumbing, electrics, insulation and security in a new property will usually feature the latest technology.

Don't be put off by minor cracks around the property. These usually appear when the plaster dries out, although larger cracks should be investigated.

PART-EXCHANGE

When it comes to move, often the biggest headache is trying to time buying and selling so that they occur at the same time, and if you are reliant upon a chain, hoping that no links are broken by a buyer or seller dropping out.

Fortunately, if you are buying a newly built home, many housebuilders operate part-exchange schemes to eliminate these pressures. You trade in your existing property having received an offer for your house based on an immediate sale value carried out by independent professionals and can then arrange a definite completion date.

As well as eliminating the fear of your buyer dropping out at the last minute or the spectre of gazumping, there is no need to move into rented accommodation as you would if you can't match your buying and selling dates, there are no time-consuming viewings by both timewasters and potential buyers, and legal costs are likely to be lower as well. You may not achieve as high a price as if you had tried your luck and waited, but then property prices in many areas could also move the other way – downwards – in the future.

Some homebuyers worry about not getting a good price for their homes if they opt for a part-exchange, but housebuilders would be wasting their time with such a promotion if they didn't offer a fair price based on a valuation carried out by independent professionals. And even if you feel you could get a better price on the open market, if the sale falls through the resulting costs could be considerable.

BUYING OFF-PLAN

Increasing competition for new homes has meant buying a property from the developer's plans – rather than waiting until it is built – has become increasingly popular.

There can be great benefits to buying this way, which is known as buying off-plan. Developers often discount properties to get sales moving at a new development, and if prices rise steeply as word gets round and as the development takes shape, you can have a real bargain on your hands.

You also often have the choice of the best plots with the most impressive views, with the bonus of gaining extra time to save and sort out a mortgage. Another advantage is that you have far more say about how your property will look if you buy off-plan. Developers usually have a sizeable range of tiles, carpeting, colour schemes and kitchen and bathroom fittings you can choose from, and you may even be able to rearrange the layout, for example changing two bedrooms into one large room, or maybe two bathrooms into one study and a bathroom.

Typically, when you buy this way, you pay several hundred pounds as a reservation fee then a deposit of 5 or 10 per cent of the purchase price a month or so after agreeing to buy. When the property is ready to move in, the remaining 90 per cent is paid.

When buying off-plan, bear in mind that if the property market contracts, completed homes could cost less than those previously bought off-plan. Check that the developer is financially sound by obtaining a report on the company from Companies House (**www.companies-house.gov.uk**).

Prepare for delays. Factors like bad weather or planning hold-ups can cause the development to run behind schedule. Examine the developer's plans carefully and refer to them on completion: are neighbouring houses too close or will you have great views of the dustbins?

Consider having a clause included in the contract that allows you to delay completion if there are faults in the property. And if your home is one of the first to be completed, be prepared to live on a building site for weeks or even months.

SUBSIDISED HOUSING

HOUSING BENEFIT

Housing benefit is paid to workers or claimants on a low income and who pay rent for a home that they occupy full-time, that is, they are only away from it temporarily (apart from a few specific exceptions). There is a threshold for the amount of savings you can have to qualify.

To claim you will need to produce forms such as wage slips and proof of the rent being charged. You will be required to state your relationship with other people in your home, such as lodgers, and whether they pay you rent.

If the council has proof you are cohabiting (living as a couple), it may pay less. It may visit your home to see if there are any indications that you live as a couple. It may also decide that the property is too big for your needs or the rent is too high for the locality and may therefore only pay part of your rent.

Claiming for housing benefit can affect other benefits such as income support and job seekers' allowance. Most students cannot claim housing benefit both in term times and in the holidays, and must wait until their course finishes.

EX-COUNCIL HOMES: RIGHT-TO-BUY

One good way to get on the property ladder is to buy a former council house. Ex-council properties can be good value, but you need to be aware of the problems which can be associated with them.

Since the 1980 Housing Act introduced right-to-buy legislation intended to 'empower' council tenants by allowing them to buy their homes at a significant discount, more than 1.5 million council homes have been sold, while those still rented to tenants are being transferred to housing associations.

There are currently a large number of council homes on the market and when they are initially sold privately they tend to be 15–20 per cent cheaper than comparable sized private homes, but price rises then move more in line with other houses in the locality.

Ex-council properties are generally good investments, but you have to make sure of the condition, as many were 'system built' and may contain building or structural defects. Also, if they are located on an estate with social and environmental problems, their resale value may be affected, so professional advice should be sought from a surveyor who knows the locality.

There are usually no problems obtaining a mortgage on such properties, as long as there is reasonable resale potential. When considering an ex-council home, investigate whether a high proportion of nearby council houses have been sold. This is promising. Beware if there have been several previous owners as the property may have a poor repairs record. Are there many problems in the locality like vandalism, noise disturbance, graffiti and illegal tipping? Find out who is responsible for maintenance of communal areas. Ask local estate agents about potential resale values. If the property has the same or a similar design and brick colour as private properties nearby, it is likely to hold its value better than a council property that looks distinctly different.

SHARED OWNERSHIP SCHEMES

Spectacular house price rises may be great news for homeowners, but it makes things more and more difficult for those starting out on the property ladder. One solution to the problem is to opt for a shared home ownership scheme, a part buy, part subsidised rent arrangement, operated throughout Britain by registered social landlords (R.S.L.s), usually housing associations or trusts. They are approved, regulated and part-funded by the government through the Housing Corporation, which funds over 4,000 homes on such schemes each year.

Schemes differ but on the whole offer 'key' workers and the lower paid the chance to get a foot on the property ladder. Some schemes are particularly suitable for people who earn too much to be a priority for social rented housing but too little to buy or rent on the open market.

Usually participants buy around a 50 per cent share to begin with although it can be less or more. A monthly rent is charged to the shared owner for the remaining equity owned by the housing association or trust, which is payable on top of their mortgage payment, service charge and bills.

Instead of having a large mortgage loan for the whole property hanging over them, there's generally a much smaller mortgage to pay on the share they own, which, when combined with the subsidised rent for the remaining share, adds up to a substantially cheaper monthly payment than if they had bought outright. Many lenders are happy to provide mortgages on this basis.

The intention of most shared ownership schemes is for the purchaser to buy more of the equity as time goes on, which is known as 'staircasing'. The remaining equity can be bought outright, or in stages. Many schemes restrict staircasing until one year after the owner has moved in and some may limit the amount bought at each stage.

Those eligible for shared ownership depends upon the scheme. Some, such as the 'Starter Homes Initiative', are only for key public sector workers such as nurses and teachers. Other schemes prioritise particular groups such as existing council tenants. Some schemes are open to anyone fitting specific financial criteria.

The definition of a 'key' worker in a scheme could be very specific or include jobs such as bus drivers. Some schemes specify that an applicant must live locally or within a limited radius to their workplace to qualify. Applicants are asked for proof of their income, which needs to be high enough to meet the costs of shared ownership and of moving (such as solicitors' fees) but not so high that a property could be bought without assistance.

Applicants must have no equity in any other property and a mortgage must have been approved. Some housing associations and trusts ask for an initial deposit, usually a few hundred pounds, with an application.

People from all walks of life are increasingly signing up to these schemes including professionals in expensive urban areas who find their incomes can't buy the housing they want. Yet with many workers joining schemes with the intention of increasing their share of ownership as their incomes go up, as buying further shares in the property must be at current market value, if prices rise too swiftly, this may become increasingly difficult.

More and more developments are mixed, with properties purchased via shared ownership and other subsidised housing schemes and affordable rental properties next to properties sold at the full market price, therefore reflecting the true social fabric of cities. Increasingly properties are in the most desirable areas because such developments only receive planning permission by including affordable housing schemes.

Shared ownership is likely to increase in importance as salaries continue to fail to keep pace with house price inflation, and as the supply of new houses fails to keep up with demand.

The downside is that the number of shared ownership schemes is still very small. Also, a number of schemes are built on unattractive brownfield or former industrial land. Others are hardly affordable, and even buying a 25 per cent share of some schemes is too much for most. There have also been a relatively high number of disputes concerning conveyancing problems.

Selling your share and moving on can also have its complications. It is not always easy to sell a share of ownership, or at the price hoped for. Some schemes have contracts that specify that the housing association's valuation is used or that it is allowed to nominate buyers first.

HOMEBUY

Recently a shared ownership scheme was launched allowing buyers to select a property on the open market rather than be restricted to those offered by housing associations. Buyers have to pay 75 per cent of the purchase price of the property under this scheme, Homebuy. The remainder is funded by the housing association, with no interest charged on this amount. If the property is sold, the purchaser receives 75 per cent and the housing association 25 per cent of the selling price.

The Homebuy scheme helps people to buy a home on the open market. The scheme is operated by selected registered social landlords (housing associations) in England. By helping some people to buy, the scheme frees up their homes for rent by others in housing need.

So the only people who can apply for the scheme are: existing tenants of registered social landlords and local councils; or those on housing waiting lists who are nominated by their local council as being in housing need. This helps to reduce waiting lists in areas where there is a shortage of social housing.

To apply for shared ownership schemes, you can register on a local council housing list or obtain application forms from housing associations themselves. Local councils have details of housing associations in their area.

In England, the Housing Corporation has information on the 2,200 housing associations in England. In Wales, contact the Housing Division at the Welsh Assembly in Cardiff. For schemes in Scotland contact the Scottish Federation of Housing Associations. Also take a look at **www.communitiesscotland.gov.uk**. In Northern Ireland there is information on the Northern Ireland Housing Executive website or contact the Northern Ireland Co-ownership Housing Association. Another site, **www.homes.org.uk**, has a facility to search for part-owners who have put their properties up for sale. The National Housing Federation has a shared ownership information pack.

OTHER HOUSING OPTIONS

BOATS

You'd like to live in a place in the country. Maybe Warwickshire or Argyll, Avon or Oxfordshire. You like the idea of city living too: perhaps Manchester, perhaps London. Buy a boat and you could live in them all.

Not only does living on a boat offer unrivalled freedom and flexibility, but it can be very cheap too. You can pick up a boat to live in for a fraction of the cost of a house. Even in the most expensive area, the centre of London, a 50 ft boat with a mooring (that's a parking space to you, landlubber) complete with mod cons like central heating, can easily come in at less than £30,000. You can still pick up canal boats for under £10,000.

Not only that but in the centre of the city boats can be surprisingly peaceful. Water deadens sound and often you're below road level and the roar of the traffic. And although the speed limit is 4 m.p.h., getting about can be quicker than sitting in traffic jams.

Many boats have most home comforts like fitted kitchens and washing machines while many marinas and boatyards offer water, sewage and electricity facilities, adequate car parking and access for emergency services.

Yet although you can buy a boat for a fraction of the price of bricks and mortar, before you splash out and join the jetty set it is important to be aware of the potential pitfalls. Could you live with cramped living quarters, high running costs, endlessly having to replace water, gas and other supplies and endure a possible lack of security or privacy? Perhaps the biggest drawback of living on a boat is the lack of space, but one of the compensations is the real community spirit amongst boat owners.

Before buying a boat have it surveyed by a marine surveyor who is a member of the Yacht Brokers, Designers and Surveyors Association, which costs from about £100–£500, and if it's older than five or six years have it taken out of the water for a full hull survey.

Residential boats are required to have a registered permanent mooring or to be continuously cruising. Around the country this cost varies greatly, depending upon location, length of boat and facilities offered at the mooring. They vary from about £40 to £200 per metre's length of the boat per year, and average around £800 per boat per year. In especially popular locations, moorings can be difficult to obtain. If the boat you wish to buy doesn't come with a mooring it's important to secure one before you buy.

Gas, electricity and solid fuel costs are negligible when compared to those of a house, but at a cost of £200 upwards the boat must be surveyed regularly, usually every four years, to obtain its Boat Safety Certificate, which is similar to an MOT certificate for a car. This typically costs £150 or so and includes over 320 checks on the engine, gas system and electrics confirming the boat's safety.

Boats should be insured, at the very least, third party insurance by law. Insurance typically costs 1 per cent of the value of the boat, and can be liable for council tax on permanent moorings.

It's vital that the vessel is adequately maintained – boats can deteriorate at a fantastic rate. If you don't look after your boat you could have serious problems with condensation, burst pipes and damp. It needs to be painted every four or five years, which could easily cost over £2,000 or £3,000 if you use a specialist firm.

Freehold and leasehold moorings are uncommon and most are based on short-term agreements that can be terminated at little notice. To be officially moored you also need planning permission from the local council and the permission of the Environment Agency and the owner of the river bank.

If you're considering applying for a conventional mortgage to buy a houseboat, forget it, as most building societies and banks wouldn't touch your application with a bargepole unless it is to be a second home, with the owner's principal home used as security. But some specialist finance companies offer marine finance, typically up to 80 per cent of the purchase price, paid back over 10–15 years.

As well as specialist boat agents, boats are advertised in magazines like *Waterways World*, *Canal Boat*, and *Canal and Riverboat*, and in *Loot* and *Exchange and Mart*.

Before you splash out and take the plunge, check the boat has a boat safety certificate; have it surveyed; use a solicitor familiar with how land law applies to boats to check things like planning consents, access, leases, mooring agreements and so on; don't buy a boat for residential use without a mooring, and lastly don't buy until you are sure the seller owns the boat – there is no log book system for boat ownership.

British Waterways has a free information pack on living on a boat, and the Residential Boat Owners' Association has a booklet, *Living Afloat*, which is £5 including p&p.

EX-COMMERCIAL PROPERTY

With good conventional residential property in increasingly short supply in many parts of the country, more and more private individuals with imagination and a spirit of adventure – rather than developers – are looking to convert commercial space into homes.

Not long ago the idea of transforming retail, industrial or office premises into residential accommodation would have appeared eccentric to many people. It would have taken a big leap of imagination to visualise turning a dreary, grey old office building or bleak factory unit into a fabulous, unusual, spacious home.

Ample opportunities to tap into the commercial conversion craze appear daily. Increasingly in cities, centrally located offices are being abandoned by companies for cheaper properties on the outskirts of the town. And as more and more of us buy off the Internet and at out-of-town superstores, city and town centre shops are becoming vacant.

Most planning departments will be receptive to conversion from commercial to residential use if the building is no longer commercially viable and is suitable for conversion.

Jobs like rewiring and plumbing for a sizeable commercial property are likely to cost far more than for a house, and it may be sensible to split the central heating system so the whole building doesn't have to be heated at one time.

Obtaining a mortgage is not always straightforward. A higher than average mortgage deposit may be required. Approaching a mortgage broker may be more profitable than one of the high street building society chains.

It can be easy to take on too much. An old warehouse may look irresistible but the conversion, refurbishing and running costs could be exorbitant.

Yet ex-commercial properties have many advantages. They often have excellent transport links. Unlike private vendors, who on the whole are principally interested in obtaining the highest price possible, owners of commercial property are usually concerned about other factors, such as obtaining a speedy sale and therefore bargains can be common.

Good sources of suitable properties are commercial property agents, auctions and the classified ads in *Estates Gazette*. The property portfolio manager at the head office of national companies may also be able to provide a list of properties for sale. If you find a suitable property but are unclear as to ownership, the Land Registry can provide details of registered owners for a small sum.

When buying a commercial property, allow plenty of time for bureaucracy: in practice tasks like obtaining planning permission, observing building regulations and delicensing a pub invariably take far longer than novices estimate.

Before committing yourself to purchase, sound out the local planning and building control officers, who may be able to pinpoint serious pitfalls from an early stage.

Be prepared for conflicts between the requirements of building control and conservationists: for example a listed building will have to retain its historical features while incorporating modern safety and energy-efficient ones.

Bear in mind the internal configuration of many commercial buildings is unsuitable for residential use which could be very costly to change. Research all possible ways of recouping costs. It may be possible to sell off sections of the property as self-contained homes, while original pub fittings, cinema seats and so on could be valuable.

Check the tax implications with the Inland Revenue and Customs and Excise. If it is not legally made clear that a building has changed from a business to residental use, income tax and VAT could become an issue.

FARM BUILDINGS

In rural areas, cash-strapped farmers are selling off barns and other farm buildings. Village pubs, shops and post offices are closing at a ferocious rate. Five or six village shops close each week, according to the Village Retail Services Association.

HOTELS

Smaller hotels are being increasingly snapped up by private buyers eager to turn them into homes. Ex-residential and care homes are increasingly becoming available as stringent legislation makes them less commercially viable. Although the larger ones will be most suitable for conversion by developers, in the right location, smaller ones could make an ideal, spacious family home.

BANKS

Banks are another option for prospective commercial property converters. More than 4,000 branches have closed in the UK from 1992–2002 and the trend continues as the public increasingly relies upon telephone and on-line banking and cashpoints. Although the chance of being granted change of use is good, look at the title documents to see if there are any restrictions to changing to residential use.

Look at the building carefully to see if it will be easy to convert. A bank may have a large vault that may cost more than the property is worth to remove. If there are offices you may have to substantially change the services. Bear in mind you'll probably be living on a busy high street. If the bank forms part of a row made up exclusively of retail outlets in a popular shopping area, it could prove difficult to turn the building into a home.

PUBS

Pubs are often ideal to convert into homes and as brewery chains often dispose of them fifty or a hundred at a time, bargains can be common, although there are plenty of potential pitfalls.

It is vital to check with the local planners that it will be possible to delicense the pub. It is a good idea to make the sale on the condition that it will be possible to delicense.

Pubs typically have enough space when restructured to turn into several spacious self-contained flats. Basements and ground floors can be particularly suitable as studios. Historically, pubs were usually more solidly built than the surrounding houses and are often full of character and have a rich past. When they are built on a corner site they're more likely to enjoy the sun throughout the day.

But it's good to bear in mind that many pubs are situated on busy main roads and many failed ones are in depressed, run down areas. Of course, before buying a property as sizeable as a pub the refurbishment and running costs have to be considered very carefully. Many pubs are offered for sale in a relatively poor condition, so obtain as extensive a survey as possible.

CHURCHES

Church congregations have been shrinking sharply in recent decades, and although this is far from welcome news at the ecclesiastical job centre, it gives homebuyers a heavenly choice of unusual, spacious properties to choose from.

Since the 1969 Pastoral Measure, reorganising Church of England Parishes, more than 1,500 Anglican churches have been considered in excess of needs and many have been bought for residential conversion. The situation has been further helped by a church-building boom a century ago, which left many parishes overstocked.

Converting a church into a home enables the creation of a wonderfully imaginative and original living space. The wealth of striking architectural features many churches possess, such as stained glass windows, grand arches, high vaulted ceilings and deep stone mullions, ensure a property that couldn't be more removed from the uniformity of a typical modern home.

But don't assume you'll be able to convert the font into an inspired bird bath or kitchen sink, or turn the pulpit into a drinks cabinet. Before selling former places of worship, the Church often removes such items.

And there can be strict stipulations over what building work can be done, especially as many such buildings have listed building status or specific conditions laid down by the Church.

If you do not plan to buy an already-converted church be prepared for the bureaucracy. Many religious conversions involve public consultation, deconsecration, listed building planning consent and consultation with English Heritage, the Advisory Board of Redundant Churches and similar organisations. And if there are bats in the belfry they are legally protected and cannot be evicted.

Worth knowing is that most first-time sales of vicarages and rectories are not liable for stamp duty.

SAVE Britain's Heritage has published *A Question of Conversion*, a guide to sympathetic redevelopment of religious buildings. Architectural salvage firms are an excellent source of fixtures, fittings and furniture salvaged from redundant churches. These include Lassco and Pew Corner. The Church Commissioners has details of church properties for sale.

ECOLOGICAL BUILDING TECHNIQUES

Architects of the future can learn a lot by looking at the techniques of the past. Underground, rammed earth, mud and straw homes date back centuries and can provide significant advantages over building with concrete and steel.

Such homes are all making a comeback in the UK as homeowners search for cheaper, more sustainable and more striking designs. Yet they often face substantial problems from building control departments and the building industry, sceptical of their potential.

The Centre for Alternative Technology in Powys runs courses and has information on and examples of ecological building techniques.

RAMMED EARTH HOMES

Earth, the world's most ancient building material, has many advantages. It is not a burnt material, so it does not emit CO_2. Concrete, on the other hand, is globally responsible for 10 per cent of carbon dioxide emissions. Earth is cheap and abundant, returns to its natural state on demolition, has low toxicity, absorbs noise and reduces fire risk. It also has a high thermal mass and therefore can slash heating bills. The relative humidity in such buildings is perfect for a healthy respiratory system.

Using rammed earth involves a simple process, with the soil and water mixture moulded and then left to dry out. It can be left to weather naturally, finished with sand or plastered over. There's plenty of proof around the world testifying to its longevity.

The In Situ Rammed Earth Company has used rammed earth to build more than one hundred buildings.

EARTH-SHELTERED HOMES

If planners want to create attractive, new, environmentally friendly homes they should watch the children's programme, *Teletubbies*. They live in an earth building, the sort of structure that can be hidden into the environment rather than be an eyesore, and which can be built cheaply from local materials.

Although underground earth shelters were last popular around the time of the woolly mammoth, they are gaining in popularity and there are now around 6,000 in the US, 1,000 in Australia and several hundred around Europe.

A shelter built into the ground has the advantages of no noise, no draughts, no damp and no nosey neighbours. They conserve energy. Some things are more expensive, like waterproofing and insulation, but many are cheaper. They require no outside decoration and are virtually maintenance free. You can make earth shelters very light if you put in side lights and roof lights.

www.earth-house.com is an informative website.

STRAW HOMES

Straw homes pre-date the mediaeval era and are energy efficient and environmentally friendly. Because straw is a waste product of farming, it is readily available and cheap.

You can even build a straw home yourself using friends and family, or enlist the experts, such as Yorkshire-based Amazon Nails, an all-women building firm specialising in straw-bale construction. A home for a family of five would cost from about £35,000.

The bales are laid in courses like ordinary bricks and wooden pins are hammered into the bales at regular intervals. A timber frame is often used. The bales can be plastered inside and out but as the walls need to breathe, traditional lime or clay plaster is used rather than cement. They are not a fire hazard because the bales are compressed so tightly there's not enough air inside to fuel combustion. The density of the bales also deters damp and mice. The bales also take the weight of the roof.

Straw homes provide massive heat and sound insulation and are very in tune with the environment. Because sustainable materials are used, they are low impact buildings. They can last as long as brick houses, and in the States some are a hundred years old.

SELF-BUILD

While hit TV shows like *Changing Rooms* and *Home Front* have encouraged many DIY'ers to tackle increasingly challenging projects, there is a growing band of handymen and women who are going for the ultimate: building their own home.

It is estimated that over 25,000 people now build their homes each year, and there is even a comprehensive self-build course at the Worcester College of Technology.

Self-builders typically make savings of 25 to 35 per cent by building their homes themselves, although the term 'self-build' is itself rather misleading. Only about 1 per cent of self-builders undertake any of the building work themselves, with most employing a builder to carry out the work for them.

One of the biggest obstacles a self-builder faces is finding a suitable building plot: one that is the right size, an affordable price and unencumbered by insurmountable planning permission problems.

Plotfinder has around 3,500 plots throughout the UK on its land and renovation database. The monthly self-build magazines, *Homebuilding and Renovating*, *Build It* and *Self-Build and Design* also detail plots, as does the Self-Build Advisory Service's website, **www.plotsearch.co.uk**.

Apart from the huge financial savings you can make by opting for self-build, it's the freedom you have to design your own home exactly how you want it that attracts most people. Recent research by *Build It* magazine indicates that 57 per cent of homeowners would rather have a home designed and built from scratch than renovate an old property.

If you opt for self-build, incorporate at least a 15 per cent contingency fund into your budget for the unexpected, which invariably will come up. Pay your builder in stages, not upfront, otherwise you won't have a hold over him if there's a dispute. Timber-framed homes, such as those offered in kit form by self-build companies, speed up the building process.

More and more lenders consider funding self-build projects. The Self-Build Advisory Service in conjunction with the Bradford and Bingley, for example, offers the Accelerator mortgage for self-builders, providing customers with a borrowing capacity of 95 per cent on the cost of the land and 95 per cent on the estimated value of the completed home, provided in advance.

The monthly self-build magazines have their own websites: *Homebuilding and Renovating* (**www.homebuilding.co.uk**); *Build It* (**www.self-build.co.uk**); *Self Build and Design* (**www.selfbuildanddesign.com**).

PROPERTIES FOR SPECIFIC BUYERS

COMMUTER HOMES

Selecting the right location is even more crucial for a commuter than it is for an ordinary homebuyer. Above all else, the property has to be close to fast and reliable transport links that lead to the source of employment.

Lots of questions need to be asked before deciding upon the suitability of a commuter home. There may be plenty of peak-time trains, but what about off-peak? If you stay in town for the evening, will you miss the last train home? Your mortgage payments may reduce by moving away from the city, but will the cost of an annual rail ticket cancel these savings out?

Property in prime commuting areas can be very price-sensitive. Prices generally rise sharply within the magic fifteen minute drive of the station, and homes near faster railway services command higher property values.

HOMES FOR THE DISABLED

Moving home is a difficult job at the best of times but when a member of the family is disabled a number of other factors creep into the equation. Fortunately, there are a number of ways homes can be built and adapted to make life easier for the disabled person and others in the family.

Relevant charities and support groups, such as the Royal National Institute for the Blind (R.N.I.B.) and the cerebral palsy charity Scope, can advise on selecting and furnishing a suitable property. The John Grooms Association for Disabled People is the largest provider of wheelchair-accessible housing in the UK with around 1,000 properties nationwide.

Wheelchair-accessible housing will typically have features like ramps, wide doorways, a wheelchair lift and lowered light switches. The majority of blind people can see something even if it is just light perception, and so a suitable home may have sound and textile clues to tell the person exactly where they are in the house, and bright colours such as yellows and blues, two colours that the visually impaired can often see.

The amount of government funding for this kind of housing has been decreasing and there is now a huge shortfall of wheelchair-accessible housing. Financial considerations are not the most important criteria when applying for a John Grooms property, and a person does not need to be in receipt of state benefits. The main criterion is that a person or someone in the family is a full-time wheelchair user who would benefit from the home. People can apply directly to John Grooms or are nominated by their local authority.

Many disabled people or their carers buy equipment to adapt their homes themselves, as they feel they can no longer rely on the NHS or charitable organisations to provide the help. Gordon Ellis and Co is a specialist company that supplies equipment under the 'Derby' brand name that can be used to adapt a conventional home, including bathroom safety equipment, grab bars, bottle openers, kettle tippers and chair and bed raisers.

Non-specialist housebuilders can also do a lot to help the disabled, especially if the home is being bought off-plan or is early in the building process. The housebuilder may be able to modify the home, for example by building ramps and making hallways wider.

PROPERTY FOR STUDENTS

Over half of the one million full-time students in England and Wales live in privately rented accommodation, and many of them stay in properties that are at best bad value for money, and at worst, plain dangerous.

Indeed, the Chartered Institute of Environmental Health recently warned that many students could be living in 'death trap' housing, forced to rent houses from private landlords who fail to make adequate safety checks. Common dangers include faulty gas appliances releasing toxic fumes, hazardous electrics and inadequate means of escape from fire.

Students no longer qualify for housing benefit and the National Union of Students notes that annual accommodation costs exceed the maximum grant in some areas. Students typically spend a whopping 55 per cent of their income on rent.

But with the help of family to obtain a mortgage, and a little planning, many of these students could bag accommodation that's not only safe, but rent-free if they let out spare rooms to pay off the mortgage costs. There may also be a big capital gain when it comes to sell.

The idea has becoming so popular that some lenders offer special mortgages for parents. Usually, a parent or another relative has to guarantee payments if the student cannot. Students clubbing together for a property should be avoided as it can result in legal pitfalls, ownership disputes and wary lenders.

Yet any parent thinking of taking on a mortgage so that their son or daughter is able to avoid a succession of poky garrets and draughty bedsits should examine the pros and cons carefully before taking the plunge.

Check with the university/college student accommodation office about the local housing and rental markets, typical rents and suitable locations. It's important to consider the location and condition of the property because if the market stagnates it may be difficult to sell, especially in a typical student area. And a house full of boisterous students is likely to receive more than average wear and tear, meaning higher repair bills.

There are ownership options to consider – parents, the student or a family trust, for example. Will the mortgage company allow you to rent or sub-let? There are tax implications to investigate, for example capital gains tax is liable on second residences. You want the purchase structured so that rent and other expenses can be offset against borrowing, and capital gains liability minimised. Capital appreciation could be offset against the annual joint allowances for a husband and wife.

If the student is the owner, the Inland Revenue's Rent-a-Room allowance can be claimed on the first £4,250 (or £81.73 per week) from lodgers, and a student owner with no other income would not pay tax on rent for the first £4,195 earned from rent, and expenses can be offset against this.

BUYING A FLAT

Buying a flat has a number of advantages over buying a house. It may enable you to live in a nicer area because flats are generally cheaper than houses. The outside of the building, communal areas and gardens are usually maintained by the managing agents and you share the costs with the other leaseholders. There may be added security as other flatowners are likely to keep an eye on your property in your absence.

Yet there are disadvantages. An inefficient managing agent can be a real headache, especially if there is a pressing problem that needs to be attended to and they don't appreciate the urgency. You may have little control and be lumbered with hefty maintenance charges.

THE LEASEHOLD SYSTEM

Most flats and a few houses are sold on a lease. The leasehold system, operated in England and Wales, can be complicated. If you 'buy' a leasehold property you do not own it, but have bought the right to live there for however long is left on your lease. The building, ground it is built upon, garden and grounds are owned by the freeholder, who is your landlord. The freeholder could be an individual, a company or your local council.

Before you are committed to buy, read the lease and go through any items you don't understand with your solicitor, who should highlight any points he thinks could cause problems. The lease may have important legally enforceable restrictions such as banning pets or restricting access to part of the grounds, so make sure you have understood every clause.

Leaseholders pay a ground rent annually to the landlord or their managing agent. It is generally a relatively small sum, from a few pounds to several hundred. The service charges, on the other hand, can be high and usually include a contribution towards things like repairs and maintenance, communal electricity and buildings insurance.

Before buying a leasehold property it's a good idea to ask for copies of the service charge demands for the last few years. Have the charges risen sharply, or have there been a high number of costly repairs?

Managing agents are not regulated by any statutory body and standards vary greatly. Before buying try to speak to other leaseholders to see whether there have been any problems concerning them.

It is important to pay the ground rent and service charges due on a leasehold property, as the freeholder is able to go to court to repossess a property if the leaseholder fails to. Therefore, for a debt of a few pounds, the freeholder would be able to take control of a property worth thousands or even hundreds of thousands of pounds.

If you feel your landlord or their managing agent has charged you too much for repairs and maintenance or for the service charge, you can challenge them through a Leasehold Valuation Tribunal. Their services are designed to be inexpensive and without the need of using a solicitor. Contact the Leasehold Enfranchisement Advisory Service for more details.

A lease can run from anything between 1 and 999 years. Many leases last for 99 years when granted and if there is still at least 70 years left to run, most lenders are happy to grant a mortgage. Any less and there may be a problem.

You can often extend the lease and what you pay the freeholder generally depends upon the property, location and the amount of time left on the lease. You would be liable for both your and the freeholder's costs and would usually need to engage a solicitor and a specialist valuer.

It is possible to buy the freehold collectively with a majority of the other leaseholders. This can be a costly and lengthy process, especially if your landlord is unwilling to sell, but adds value to the property and should reduce service and maintenance charges for each flat. There are a number of rules to navigate concerning things like ground rent, the type of building and how long residents have lived in their flats. Again, you would need to engage a solicitor and freehold valuer.

COMMONHOLD

The 2002 Commonhold and Leasehold Reform Act (which is likely to come into operation in late 2003 at the earliest) introduces a new form of land ownership, commonhold, aimed at increasing rights and protection to the country's (except for Scotland, which already has a commonhold system) two million leaseholders. Based on the condominium system in North America, this form of tenure provides a new means of owning a flat, where you do not have a finite lease that usually only can be extended at considerable expense.

The antiquated leasehold system allows the freeholder the power to make all decisions on maintenance and repairs while the leaseholder foots the bill. With commonhold, flat owners have total ownership of their properties and also share in the common parts of the building and running of the block.

A commonhold estate consists of a group of freehold properties such as a group of flats in a block as well as an extra freehold title for the common or communal parts, given to a commonhold association owned and controlled by the freeholders. The association is responsible for such things as maintenance, repair and insurance of the common parts. A single commonhold community statement replaces the need for separate leases.

Commonhold applies to new-build developments, and lessees who have jointly acquired the freehold interest in their properties may convert to the commonhold system if the minimum requirements of the Act are met.

USEFUL TELEPHONE NUMBERS/ EMAIL ADDRESSES

PARK HOMES

Park Home and Caravan: 01622 778778

THATCHED HOMES

Specialist insurers of thatched homes include NFU Mutual (0845 603 0521), Churchill Insurance Company (0800 200345) and Country Thatch Insurance (01206 771333).

RESTORATION AND REFURBISHMENT

Retailers of architectural salvage are on the Architectural Salvage Index (01483 203221) and further information is available from Salvo (01890 820333, **www.salvo.co.uk**).

BOATS

Collidge and Partners: 01843 295295 (finance)
Virginia Currer Marine: 01753 832312 (agents)

EX-COMMERCIAL PROPERTY

Estate agents specialising in commercial property include
Sidney Phillips (01981 250333); Fleurets (020 7636 8992);
Christie and Co (020 7227 0700) and Robert Barry and Co (01285
641642).

CHURCHES

Lassco: 020 7739 0448
Pew Corner: 01483 533337

RAMMED EARTH HOMES

In Situ Rammed Earth Company:
rowland@earth.netkonect.co.uk

EARTH-SHELTERED HOMES

Futura Homes: 020 8553 6776

STRAW HOMES

Amazon Nails: 01706 814696

SELF-BUILD

Boarder Oak: 01568 708752
Plotfinder: 01527 834439
Potton Homes: 01767 263300
Worcester College of Technology: 01905 619031

HOMES FOR THE DISABLED

Gordon Ellis and Co: 01332 810504
John Grooms Association for Disabled People: 020 7452 2000
Royal National Institute for the Blind: 0845 766 9999
Scope: 0808 800 3333

MONEY MATTERS

WHAT CAN YOU AFFORD?

Although there are an increasing number of exceptions, mortgage lenders will generally lend around three times an individual's salary (or around 2.5 a couple's joint salary) but there are lots of other one-off and ongoing costs to consider before deciding how much you can afford.

On top of the purchase price there are regular outgoings that could include electricity, gas, water rates, council tax, service charges, buildings and contents insurance and telephone. You should also factor in other costs like running a car, commuting, entertaining, food and drink, life assurance and pension provision.

Also think ahead to changed circumstances. Are you planning to start a family or enlarge your present one, which could mean the loss of one partner's income?

AFFORDABILITY CALCULATION

1) **Total net monthly income (after tax and national insurance deductions)**
2) **Monthly outgoings (everything from the supermarket bill to transport and club subscriptions)**
3) **Potential increase in monthly outgoings if you move (running costs or commuting costs may be greater, for example)**
4) **Monthly mortgage payment on new home**

Add 2, 3 and 4 together and subtract the total from 1. There should be some money left over for holidays, emergencies and so on. You will also have to budget for the one-off costs of buying.

THE COST OF BUYING

There are a number of costs that need to be budgeted for when buying a home in addition to the deposit. A home costing £150,000 with a loan value of £100,000 can expect to attract costs approaching £3,000. This is made up of a mortgage valuation (£250 or so, more than double for a full survey); credit search (£15); a mortgage arrangement fee (£300 or more); conveyancing (legal costs) (£500); search fee (£150); postage and so on (£30); land registry fee (£100); stamp duty (£1,500).

If you're selling as well, the estate agent's fee (typically 2 per cent) for a £150,000 house adds another £3,000 to the bill.

A closer look at these fees:

LEGAL COSTS

Conveyancing, the legal work carried out in order to buy or sell a property, includes Land Registry and local authority searches, and for leasehold properties, examining the lease to see what service charges or special conditions apply.

SEARCH FEE

The 'search' or local authority search is usually carried out by your solicitor as part of the conveyancing process. It is a check against any future plans to establish the planning history, traffic and building plans and any restrictions attached to the property that could adversely affect the property you wish to buy. It is a precaution to prevent you from ending up with a superstore or new dual carriageway as a neighbour without knowing it, before you buy.

Planning proposals are looked for, such as changes to road layouts, building developments and alterations to land use or public rights of way, and also possible planning restrictions like including the property in a conservation area.

Searches vary in area covered, which may just be the street the property is located in, or the whole neighbourhood. Clarify with your solicitor exactly what it covers, and make further inquiries if required. Searches vary widely in price, currently from £35 to £200, depending upon the local authority they are made in.

Searches typically take ten working days, that is, a fortnight, but can take anything from under a day to several months. You can speed things up by paying extra for a 'personal search', which takes two or three days. Remember that if your property purchase drags on, the search may be considerably out of date by the time you move in.

LAND REGISTRY FEE

Your solicitor will arrange for this fee to be paid and include this in his final bill – from £40 on a £20,000 flat to £500 on a £750,000 substantial house – to have the property registered in your name.

STAMP DUTY

This is levied by the government on property transactions. There is no stamp duty on properties and land worth less than £60,000, and on properties valued at less than £150,000 it is waived where the property is within a regeneration area. The Inland Revenue website and helpline indicate where these areas are located. Stamp duty is currently charged at 1 per cent on properties worth between £60,000 and £250,000, 3 per cent on property sales above £250,000 and 4 per cent for sales above £500,000.

These thresholds increase distortions in property prices. Currently, a homebuyer paying £249,000 for a house pays £2,490 duty, while one buying a £251,000 property will pay £7,530. Because of this, many buyers are tempted to encourage sellers to reduce the asking price of their property and charge an inflated price for fixtures and fittings in compensation so that stamp duty is levied at below one of the thresholds for rate changes and so avoiding a higher rate of duty. There is reasonable leeway for doing this, but don't be tempted to apportion an unusually high sum for the fixtures and fittings as the Stamp Duty Office carefully scrutinises such practices.

SURVEYOR'S FEE

If you are taking out a mortgage, your lender will require a basic valuation on the property, typically costing around £100–£200. But it is usually a good idea to have the property further investigated to identify any potential problems it may be harbouring. A basic survey (often called a homebuyer's report) costs around £250–£400 and a full structural survey, typically costing from £400 upwards, looks into far more detail. When the government's initiative to speed up property transactions comes in, by requiring sellers to provide 'seller's packs' with documents relating to their property, a survey will be included in the pack. For more details on surveys see the Surveys section in Chapter 7.

MORTGAGE LENDER'S ARRANGEMENT FEE

Your lender may charge around £200 to £500 to cover their administration costs. Ask whether it is still payable should the sale not go through.

MORTGAGE PAYMENT PROTECTION INSURANCE (M.P.P.I.)

In theory M.P.P.I. covers your mortgage payments should you become unemployed or too ill to work. But study the small print, which could mean many claims would be refused.

MORTGAGE INDEMNITY GUARANTEE (M.I.G.)

M.I.G.s protect the lender rather than you should you run into financial difficulties and is more likely to be required from the lender the lower your deposit is. As M.I.G.s can cost as much as 9 per cent of the purchase price, it may be cheaper to take out a loan and pay a higher deposit instead.

FIXTURES AND FITTINGS

These may be included in the sale price, or you may wish to pay for some separately. The big jumps in stamp duty payable in each price threshold has caused some buyers to pay an exaggerated sum for fixtures and fittings like carpets so that the purchase price is at the cheaper rate of stamp duty. But too high a figure could cause the Inland Revenue to investigate and charge stamp duty at the higher rate.

BUILDINGS AND CONTENTS INSURANCE

Unless it is a condition of the mortgage deal, don't automatically buy your contents and buildings cover through your lender as it may be substantially cheaper elsewhere. Your lender will insist on you taking out buildings cover.

OTHER COSTS

These could include the cost of the removal van, taking goods out of storage, urgent repairs such as new locks, professional cleaning of carpets and the cost of redirecting the post. Then there's the redecorating.

THE DEPOSIT

You pay this, typically 10 per cent of the purchase price (but 5 per cent can often be negotiated), when you legally commit yourself to the purchase, at the exchange of contracts. If you have a 100 per cent mortgage the deposit is paid by your lender.

CALCULATE YOUR ONE-OFF PAYMENTS

Add these together to get an idea of the one-off costs of buying:

Estate agent's fee
conveyancing fee
stamp duty
deposit
search fees
Land Registry fee
survey
lender's fee
mortgage indemnity guarantee
removal costs
repair and redecoration
other

TOTAL

SHARING A PROPERTY TO MAKE IT MORE AFFORDABLE

TAKE IN A LODGER TO HELP PAY THE MORTGAGE

Under the government's rent-a-room scheme you can charge just over £80 per week before income tax is payable. Some mortgages allow you to take this income into account when calculating how much you can borrow.

Therefore it may be advantageous to buy a two-bed flat in a cheaper area or a bit further from the station instead of a more central one-bed to enable you to have the option of letting out a room. For more details, see Chapter 10.

COHABITING

Most couples buying a home will purchase on a joint basis and therefore will be equally liable to meet the repayments. For this reason, though hardly romantic, it is sensible to draw up a pre-purchase agreement. This arrangement could also be used in the case of two friends buying together.

Unmarried people do not have the same legal rights as those that are married. The law does not recognise such a thing as a common-law wife and therefore unmarried couples are not covered by the divorce laws. For this reason knowing who owns what and how much each person contributed to the mortgage and household expenses will make things less messy in the event of a break-up.

If you are both named on a bill or invoice you are 'jointly and severally' liable for the debt, which means that if you split up and your partner is uncontactable, you can be pursued for the full amount owed, not just your half. Joint liability applies to any debt where you both sign up to the agreement, whether they be overdrafts, loans or hire purchase agreements. If you did not sign the agreement but contributed to payments, on a hire purchase say, you are not legally liable. Similarly, if you share a credit card but are the secondary rather than primary cardholder, only the primary cardholder is responsible for the debt.

Any pre-purchase agreement you make should state whether each party owns a fifty-fifty share of the property or otherwise, the amount of deposit each paid, what will happen if one of you is later unable to pay the mortgage, and establish who would be responsible for the payment of certain bills. It could state that in the event of the relationship breaking down, one side has the right to buy out the remaining party.

IF YOU SPLIT UP

If the relationship breaks down and your mortgage is in joint names, your responsibilities and rights are identical whether you are sharing, cohabiting or married.

It is important to notify relevant organisations about your change in circumstances. If you are staying on at the property, you will need to take on the sole responsibility for things like utility bills and insurances. If you are a primary credit card holder, cancel your partner's card. If you are now the sole occupier of the property, contact your local authority as you are entitled to receive a 25 per cent discount on your council tax bill.

Your mortgage lender may be able to help with a remortgage if you want to buy out your partner's share of the property. You need to establish the property's worth, with a surveyor's valuation. The person wanting to keep the property would need to pay the other party their deposit and half of the increase to do this. The lender will not necessarily agree to this as they may doubt your ability to pay for the loan alone. But if there is no problem a solicitor would draw up new documents and have them registered at the Land Registry.

BUYING AS A GAY COUPLE

Gay couples should have no problems buying a property and lenders will treat your finances as they would for any other unmarried couple. As partners have no legal rights, draw up a will if you want your partner to inherit the property in the event of your death.

Problems have arisen relating to the granting of life and critical illness insurance in the past, however. See the Insurance section in Chapter 6 for more details.

BUYING JOINTLY WITH FRIENDS

Property prices have risen so sharply in many areas of Britain in recent years that buying a property jointly with a friend or friends is the only way many singletons can now get on the housing ladder.

Lenders are less wary about this type of arrangement than in the past and typically will lend a multiple (usually three times) of one salary and one times the others to a maximum of four. Legally a maximum of four people can own a property together.

It is important to draw up a legally binding agreement to cover the potential problems that could later arise. If you are taking out a joint mortgage this is especially important as each of you is responsible for the whole loan if something goes wrong. You don't want to be stuck with a huge mortgage as your mate decides to jack in his job and hitchhike to Timbuktu. Would the rest of you be able to take up his share of the mortgage or would you have to sell?

There is the possibility that you may be buying the property in one person's name only, maybe because the other person (or people) in the arrangement has a low or irregular income or is self-employed without a sufficient track record for lending purposes. This would mean that those not named as owning the property would have to sign away their rights to the property.

Before taking the step of buying with friends, try living with them first in rented accommodation. If one turns out to be an insomniac dance music addict who only pays the bills when the bailiffs come knocking and last did the washing up when Thatcher was prime minister, and you're quiet and reclusive, have always kept your finances in perfect order and like the place spotlessly clean, maybe tying yourselves to a property and mortgage isn't the best idea.

If you do go ahead, draw up the details of the pre-purchase legal document before visiting a solicitor so that you do not run up big bills arguing over them in his office. The agreement should include the percentage of the mortgage each party will pay, how much each of you has paid towards the deposit and how the property would be divided if you needed to sell.

Circumstances often change, especially if you are in your twenties. You may marry or change jobs and have to relocate, so the contract should make allowance for this, and give each party the right to ask for the property to be sold, for any reason and whenever they want.

It should be made clear in the agreement how this would be done. Who would pay for the sale? Would the value of the property be agreed by asking an estate agent to value it before the share is sold? Any parties that opt to stay should have the opportunity of buying out those who are leaving.

A joint savings account into which everyone pays their monthly contribution, or some other simple system should be put in place for the mortgage payments and other regular charges relating to the property.

Lastly, all parties should have life insurance, and preferably critical illness insurance also, in place when you buy.

JOINT TENANTS OR TENANTS IN COMMON?

A property can be owned jointly in different ways:

- **Joint tenancy agreement – In this case two or more people own equal shares of the property and if one party dies the survivor/s automatically receive/s their share. This way is usually used by cohabiting or married couples.**
- **Tenancy in common – Here, if one of the tenants in common dies, their rights pass to their next of kin or whoever is nominated to receive the rights to their share of the property in their will.**
- **Declaration of trust and cohabitation agreement – Here, the percentage of the property each party owns is specified, which may not be equal if there are different salaries involved or one party paid a larger deposit, for example. It can include details such as who owns the refrigerator in the kitchen if it is being shared. Upon death each share can be left to anyone. This method is suitable for both cohabiting couples and friends buying jointly.**

OTHER WAYS TO MAKE BUYING YOUR FIRST HOME EASIER

FOCUS ON UP-AND-COMING LOCATIONS

There's better value in areas where the potential has not yet been exploited.

CONSIDER A SHARED OWNERSHIP SCHEME

You buy a percentage of your home from a housing association and pay a subsidised rent on the remainder. You can buy some or all of the rest as and when you can afford it. Contact local housing associations for details. There are more details in the section on Subsidised housing in Chapter 4.

BUY A BOAT

Houseboats can be picked up for a fraction of the cost of a house or flat and moorings can be obtained in the centre of town. There are more details in the section about buying a boat in Chapter 4.

SELF-BUILD

Finding a plot and organising the building of your own home can save a considerable sum. There are more details in the Self-build section in Chapter 4.

RENOVATE OR REFURBISH

Search out a bargain by doing extra legwork contacting agents, trawling the net and auction catalogues.

FIND A GUARANTOR

Parents and other relatives who have benefited from rising property values and who therefore may have considerable equity in their own homes are increasingly acting as guarantors to enable their children to get a larger first mortgage to get a first foothold on the housing ladder. Some guarantor mortgage schemes require the guarantor only to guarantee the shortfall between the amount the borrower may be offered by the lender and the actual size of the loan. So if your earnings can only get you a £60,000 mortgage but the property is costing £90,000, the guarantor is only responsible for the £30,000 difference.

There can be dangers with a guarantor mortgage. If the children remain with the same lender and default on the loan fifteen or twenty years later, the parents would still be responsible for the debt. An alternative to a parent acting as guarantor is remortgaging their own property to pay the deposit on their offspring's home.

TAKE OUT A MORTGAGE WITH AN INCREASED PAYMENT TERM

Recently, lenders have been increasing payment terms on mortgages from the usual 25 years to 30 or even 40. The monthly payments are therefore lower, although you risk paying for your home well into retirement if your circumstances do not change and you do not reduce the payment term in the future.

OBTAIN A 100 PER CENT MORTGAGE

If you find it difficult to save for a deposit many lenders offer 100 per cent mortgages, although the interest rate is likely to be slightly higher than for those putting down a deposit. Borrowing the total amount for the property exposes you to a greater probability of slipping into negative equity should prices fall. Also, if you are borrowing more than 90 per cent loan to value (L.T.V.) you may have to pay a mortgage indemnity guarantee (M.I.G.), covering the lender if you default on the loan. This is usually around 3 per cent of the loan but can be substantially more.

EX-LOCAL AUTHORITY PROPERTIES

These are often very good value for money.

BUYING A NEWLY BUILT HOME

Not only may there be incentives to buy such as free appliances, payment of legal fees, 'move in for £99' starter deals and other enticements, but the property is likely to have a fitted kitchen and maybe free carpeting and curtains. The property should be low maintenance, low on energy costs, have a guarantee, and be free of problems that plague old properties like damp or loose roof tiles.

6 MORTGAGES

FINDING A MORTGAGE

To be taken seriously by your seller, when you make an offer, and to reduce pressure generally, you'll want to fix up a mortgage in principle at the outset so you're armed with a certificate with a mortgage offer when you find that dream home.

But bear in mind that the offer in principle is not a guarantee that the lender will loan you the required funds. The lender could refuse for a number of reasons, for example the surveyor could value the property for less than you wish to borrow; you could have taken on further loans since obtaining the certificate, making you a greater credit risk; or your income may have fallen. If you apply for a 'mortgage in principle' certificate, ask the lender under which circumstances would they pull out of the deal.

CHOOSING A MORTGAGE

The range of mortgages available has greatly increased in recent years and although this gives borrowers far more scope, the abundance of choice can make the process of selecting one rather overwhelming.

A visit to high street lenders will give you an idea of how much you can borrow and rates on offer. It's worth contacting your bank, as it may offer existing customers better borrowing power or improved interest rates. Banks may give enhanced terms to graduates who have banked with them through their student days.

Lenders often offer incentives like paying legal fees, the cost of the valuation or maybe a cashback – a one-off sum paid by the lender when the loan is granted. But watch out for hidden costs and catches. You may be tied to the lender's buildings or contents insurance or there may be onerous redemption penalties if you want to change to another lender in the future. Examine the small print carefully.

It is worth saving for a deposit (at least 5 per cent of the value of the cost of the property you intend to buy) as it gives you access to the best mortgage deals. A mortgage that requires a deposit but is 1 per cent or 2 per cent lower than one that does not will usually save far more money than the cost of the deposit in the long run.

It's a good idea to set up a savings account just for your future home. If you find this difficult, it may indicate that you would have trouble keeping up with the mortgage payments.

MORTGAGE TYPES

There are essentially two types of loan: repayment mortgages and interest-only mortgages. The most popular duration of a mortgage is 25 years, but increasingly, younger buyers are opting for loans of 30 or 35 years to reduce the monthly repayments, while older buyers often opt for 10 to 20 year loans.

Deciding the length of the mortgage isn't as crucial as it may sound, because depending upon its type and age, you can change the term or repay it early. You can also increase your borrowing, suspend payments temporarily, increase your borrowing or change to another lender.

REPAYMENT MORTGAGES

With a repayment mortgage your monthly payments gradually pay off the entire debt, both the capital you have borrowed and the interest it is attracting. You are mostly paying interest at the start, mostly capital at the end. You can make extra payments if you wish, but some lenders only reduce the mortgage annually and these extra payments may not benefit the mortgage until then. One advantage of repayment loans is their flexibility: it is often possible to extend the length of the loan if interest rates rise and you have trouble meeting the monthly payments. Currently, according to the Council of Mortgage Lenders, 80 per cent of new mortgages are repayment ones.

INTEREST-ONLY MORTGAGES

If your mortgage is interest-only, you are simply paying off the interest on the loan, and therefore at the end of the mortgage term you still owe the total amount borrowed.

You can take out a separate investment vehicle, such as an endowment or ISA, to repay the capital at the end of the mortgage term, although there is a degree of risk as the investment vehicle is likely to be linked to the stock market.

If you will have some way of paying off the loan, perhaps an inheritance, or you plan to pay off the loan when you sell, you can take the high risk option and have no savings plan running alongside the loan, but there could be considerable problems should the property go down in value.

ENDOWMENT MORTGAGES

An endowment insurance policy coupled to your mortgage allows you to invest through the company's fund managers and at the same time provides insurance cover to pay off the loan if you die before the end of the term. The amount needed to pay off the loan at the end of the term is not guaranteed and there could be a shortfall between the amount the investment earns and the amount of capital that needs to be repaid, as has happened to a number of endowment policyholders in recent years. Indeed, in May 2002 figures showed that 6 million out of Britain's 10.7 million endowments are unlikely to reach their targets. Endowment policies are costly and inflexible, and you can't cash them in early if you want to receive their full benefits.

Incidentally, if you think you have been mis-sold an endowment, visit the Consumers' Association website, **www.endowmentaction.co.uk**.

ENDOWMENT POLICIES AND GAY MEN

As endowment policies have a life insurance element, some providers will not offer endowment mortgages to gay men due to concerns about AIDS. Since the 1980s life insurance premiums for gay men have risen as life insurers' perceptions of their life expectancy fell.

Some providers therefore charge as much as three times the normal life insurance rate to gay men because of the perceived risk. Gay independent financial advisers Massow Financial Services (**www.massow.co.uk**) are experts in this area.

ISA MORTGAGES

ISA (individual savings account) mortgages are a quite new tax-efficient way of investing up to £7,000 per year. The money you put into an ISA grows tax free and you invest in shares usually through unit trusts designed to reduce the risks of the stock market. You invest in an equity ISA in either cash, stocks or life insurance up to your annual tax-free ISA allowance and pay off the capital at the end of the term with this. There is no guarantee that the ISA will pay off your loan, but if it does particularly well you can pay the mortgage off early. However, if the stock market underperforms when you want to pay off the loan, you will have to wait for share prices to recover.

Unlike an endowment policy, there is no built-in life insurance with an ISA mortgage, they do not have a fixed term and are therefore flexible should your plans change.

PENSION MORTGAGES

You can also opt for a pension mortgage, if you have a personal pension policy. Your mortgage and personal pension plan are linked and when the mortgage term ends the tax-free lump sum from your pension is used to pay off the outstanding capital. You therefore are able to use the income tax credits of a pension in addition to those on the interest of your loan. But the amount you have left with which to retire is reduced.

This is a very tax-efficient way to repay your mortgage, especially if you are a higher rate taxpayer.

FLEXIBLE MORTGAGES

Flexible mortgages have surged in popularity – accounting for 8 per cent of mortgages in 1998–1999 and 20 per cent in 2002 in England, according to the Survey of English Housing and the Office of the Deputy Prime Minister.

They vary, but can permit you to borrow back money, take payment holidays, make underpayments and overpayments. Some can be used as current accounts where you in effect are paying off a huge overdraft. They generally incur a higher interest rate than standard home loans but interest is charged on a daily basis and you could potentially pay your mortgage off early, and borrowing back money you have already paid is cheaper than taking out a personal loan.

SELF-CERTIFICATION MORTGAGES

These are suitable for self-employed people having trouble with standard mortgage lenders who want earnings proved via pay slips or at least two years' accounts. They are offered on the basis of the applicant stating their likely income rather than proving their past income with documentary evidence. Sometimes an accountant is required to back up your statement. Because there is a higher risk, the interest rate is generally higher than for a standard mortgage. In addition, the deposit required is higher and loan to value is lower, typically 75 to 90 per cent of the value of the property.

There are currently more than fifteen lenders offering these mortgages and they are becoming increasingly common and therefore increasingly competitive. Some offer payment holidays or allow you to overpay when you are able to.

ADVERSE CREDIT MORTGAGES

If you are a contract worker, have more than one job, receive a significant amount of your pay in commission, or have an adverse credit problem such as a loan default, county court judgement or are a discharged bankrupt, there are a number of lenders willing to provide adverse credit (or sub-prime or credit-impaired or non-conforming) mortgages. These, understandably, are at a higher rate than standard mortgages.

Adverse credit mortgages are usually sold by mortgage brokers, although some of the larger lenders have their own specialist divisions under a different brand name offering such mortgages. If you use a broker, ensure that they are regulated by the mortgage code.

Most lenders will consider cutting the interest rate or a switch to a standard loan if the borrower keeps up a good payment record. Most adverse credit mortgages require a 5 or 10 per cent deposit and are subject to redemption penalties.

CASHBACK MORTGAGES

Some mortgages offer a cash sum when the loan starts. Although this can be handy at such an expensive time, if there is a more competitive mortgage on offer it will save far more money in the long run.

MORTGAGE INDEMNITY GUARANTEE

If you borrow more than 75 per cent of the cost of the property, you may be required to buy an insurance policy called a mortgage indemnity guarantee (M.I.G.) which covers the lender if you do not pay the mortgage.

100 PER CENT MORTGAGES

More and more lenders permit homebuyers to borrow the full purchase price of the property, where no deposit is required. Although this bypasses having to save for a deposit, you are borrowing to the limit and have no leeway and therefore it can cause considerable problems should the value of the property fall below the mortgage amount (known as negative equity) as it can make it very difficult to sell and leave you trapped in a property you want to leave, even though you could afford something better.

Then again, raising a deposit on the property you wish to buy can be difficult and delaying buying because of this could mean property prices rising substantially in the meantime. A 100 per cent mortgage could be a way around this.

MORTGAGE RATES

When you have decided upon your type of mortgage there are a variety of rates to choose from. To minimise risk go for a repayment mortgage with a fixed or capped rate.

STANDARD VARIABLE RATE

If you opt for this kind of mortgage, your monthly repayments will be at the lenders' normal rate, which is usually about 1.75 per cent above the base rate set by the Bank of England. If the Bank's base rate increases or decreases, it will too. They are often the most expensive option, but good for borrowers when interest rates are coming down.

Discounted, fixed and capped mortgage deals revert to the standard variable rate when the deal finishes.

DISCOUNTED RATE

Here you pay a rate of interest set below the lender's standard variable rate – which could change – for a specified period. It follows the variable rate, and therefore could go down further or move upwards if rates change. For example, if the standard rate is 6 per cent and the discounted rate is 2 per cent, you pay 4 per cent. If the standard rate goes up to 7 per cent, you pay 5 per cent and so on. After the discounted period the loan reverts to the variable rate. Redemption penalties usually apply.

FIXED RATE

Here you fix the interest rate you are paying for a set period, usually between one and five years. Your monthly repayments remain the same during this time regardless of whether interest rates in the economy as a whole rise or fall. This is a boon for budgeting as you know exactly what you will be paying for the specified period. You benefit if rates rise, but if they fall, you can lose out. In this instance changing to another mortgage with a better rate may not be economical if you have to pay a redemption penalty to free yourself from the loan. The redemption penalty generally reduces further into the loan.

Beware of loans that impose a redemption penalty after the fixed rate period has ended. You will be paying the lender's standard variable rate and it may be too costly to move to a better deal elsewhere. You may also be required to buy the lender's buildings and/or contents insurance with this sort of loan, which may not be competitively priced.

CAPPED RATE

Capped rate mortgages are designed to give you the best of both worlds: the opportunity to benefit from lower rates but only rises to a set limit. These mortgages therefore follow interest rates downwards, but there is a specified upper limit above which the rate cannot go. They are generally lower than the standard variable rate but not as competitive as some discounted or fixed rates. The arrangement is for a set period, usually two or three years. These mortgages are most suitable if there is uncertainty about whether rates will be going up or down, or if they are rising quickly. As with fixed rate mortgages, redemption penalties often apply.

INCOME MULTIPLES

As a general rule, single borrowers can usually borrow three times their salary, and up to four times if they can provide a deposit of at least 10 per cent.

Joint borrowers can typically borrow 2.5 times the joint incomes or three times the main income and one times the second income. A 10 per cent deposit may push this up to four times the main income or three times joint.

But the mortgage world has increased greatly in recent years and there are many more lenders and products available with a great variety of lending criteria applied, so these income multiples are by no means set in stone.

BETTER CHOICE BUT BEWARE

The mortgage market has transformed completely from the days in the 1970s when mortgages were rationed by the building societies and the idea of extending your mortgage to pay off a credit card or go on holiday was unthinkable.

In recent years, with house prices in many areas rising more quickly than salaries, and with many more lenders in the marketplace launching a huge variety of mortgages and relaxing credit standards, an increasing number of mortgage companies are now routinely lending as much as five times a homebuyer's salary. Mortgage brokers can find lenders who lend more.

There's some logic to this in a property market where prices have been shooting through the roof and where interest rates are relatively low. But it spells increasing danger if the market slows down or even crashes. If rates shoot up to around 16 per cent, as in the heady days of the last housing crash, those overborrowing could be in for a devastating shock.

Many homeowners have benefited greatly from the values of their homes going up by unprecedented amounts and this is a way many people are able to borrow far more than three times their salaries. For many, the temptation to remortgage or borrow against the equity in their homes to spend on anything from cars, holidays and the high life is great and it is now possible to find lenders who will lend dizzying amounts, regardless of your salary.

Bear in mind that no one, however expert they are, can predict the interest rates of the future.

BOOSTING YOUR CHANCES OF OBTAINING A LOAN

Certain factors increase your chances of obtaining a loan. This includes being on the electoral roll (telephone your local council for an application form), not missing payments on loans and credit cards, having utility bills in your name and paying on time, having a growing savings account and being able to inform the lender of any prospect of promotion or salary increase.

CREDIT REFERENCE AGENCY FILES

If you have problems obtaining a loan you can request a copy of your credit file from the credit reference agencies.

The file, costing £2, shows the information held about you and where it has been obtained from. Write, sending this amount along with the addresses you have lived at in the last six years. If the file contains incorrect information or information about other people with which you have no financial connection, you can ask for the entry to be removed, corrected or for a note to be put on the file explaining why you think the information is wrong.

The Data Protection Commissioner can provide a leaflet explaining how to request changes on your credit reference file.

COUNTY COURT JUDGEMENTS (C.C.J.S)

C.C.J.s can be a matter of concern to a lender as it demonstrates that someone had to take you to court to get you to pay up. But

C.C.J.s are increasingly common these days and also many lenders have relaxed their lending criteria in recent years.

If you receive a C.C.J., you can ask the court to remove the judgement if you can pay the debt within 28 days. Write to the court concerned, speak to its officials or contact your local Citizen's Advice Bureau.

To see whether any county court judgements are registered against your name, send £4.50 to the Registry Trust for a postal search of the register for each name and address searched.

INDEPENDENT FINANCIAL ADVISERS

More than half of mortgages are now arranged through independent financial advisers. I.F.A.s are obliged by the Financial Services Act to live up to their name and give customers the advice most suitable for their circumstances.

To find I.F.A.s in your area, call Independent Financial Advice Promotion or the Independent Financial Advice Bureau.

MORTGAGE BROKERS

You could contact a mortgage broker, who may or may not also be an independent financial adviser, and who may be able to source more competitive mortgages, more borrowing power, or help where things are not straightforward, such as if you are self-employed or have had an adverse credit history.

Although brokers earn commission from lenders, many charge borrowers too – typically a flat fee or a percentage of the loan – but it's worth asking whether they will waive this fee, which many are willing to do in this highly competitive field.

It's important to find a reputable, independent broker with access to a wide range of lenders, and who can sort through unsuitable products until they find what is best for you. They may be able to obtain favourable deals on loans, such as waiving of valuation fees. They work within a mortgage code, so read it to check you are getting the service you are entitled to.

WHEN THINGS GO WRONG

MISSED MORTGAGE PAYMENTS   Encouraged by the Mortgage Code and the realisation that there are many reasons why borrowers may fall behind with their payments (ill health, relationship breakdowns, redundancy and so on), lenders are more understanding than in the past when this happens. The key is to communicate and be co-operative.

When one or two payments are missed the likelihood is a reminder from your lender by telephone and letter, but if you have made no response, once three payments have been missed your lender may start proceedings to repossess by applying for a court possession order. Not only would you lose your home, but you would find it difficult to borrow money in the future. If, on the other hand, you show from the start your willingness to put things right, your lender is more likely to show leniency, possibly by accepting lower payments for a while.

From the first missed payment to eviction usually takes around a year, but could be as little as eight months. If, from the first payment to the application for an eviction warrant, you manage to agree a payment schedule with your lender, the lender will usually stop the eviction proceedings. And even when a property has been repossessed, some lenders will return the keys to the borrower as long as the arrears have been cleared in full.

STEPS TO TAKE IF YOU HIT MONEY PROBLEMS Firstly, speak to your lender. As soon as you think you will have problems with repayments, tell your lender. If your lender is offering loans at a cheaper interest rate, ask whether you can transfer to that. Otherwise, ask whether your loan can be rescheduled so that your monthly payments are reduced or deferred. Pay what you can but only as much as you can afford. Your lender will prefer smaller regular payments than the promise of a larger sum that you later don't fulfil. Changing to another lender will probably be difficult as your missed payments will be revealed.

See whether you are eligible for income support. On loans taken out after September 1995, you must be out of work for nine months before it can start.

If you have a mortgage indemnity guarantee (a M.I.G., or M.I.P., for mortgage indemnity premium) because you have borrowed a large percentage of the house price, this insures the lender, rather than the borrower, if you fail to pay your debt and your lender can still pursue you for the amount owed for up to twelve years.

REPOSSESSION Examine every option to avoid having your home repossessed. Could you take on another job just for a short period to get back on track? If your home is big enough, could you temporarily cram into less rooms in the property, register with a bed and breakfast agency and let out the spare room or rooms to gain extra income? How about taking in a lodger, or remortgaging, maybe over a longer term to reduce the monthly payments?

Free advice about debt is available from the National Debt Line, as well as your local Citizen's Advice Bureau (or look at their website, **www.nacab.org.uk**). Payplan (**www.payplan.com**) and the Consumer Credit Counselling Service (**www.cccs.co.uk**) can offer in-depth debt assessments and help draft debt management programmes tailored to individual circumstances.

FINANCIAL WEBSITES

Financial websites are often a good source of information and include **www.ftyourmoney.com**, **www.thisismoney.com**, **www.finance4professionals.com**, **www.marketplace.co.uk**, **www.moneyextra.com**, **www.charcolonline.co.uk**, **www.moneygator.com**, **www.advisa-direct.co.uk**, **www.moneysupermarket.com**, **www.moneyquest.co.uk**, **www.virginmoney.com**, **www.creditweb.co.uk**, **www.simplyhomeloans.co.uk**, **www.whatmortgageonline.co.uk**, **www.mortgages-online.co.uk** and **www.freeserve.com/money**. Lenders' websites include **www.abbeynational.co.uk** (Abbey National); **www.alliance-leicester.co.uk** (Alliance and Leicester); **www.marketplace.co.uk** (Bradford and Bingley); **www.britannia.co.uk** (Britannia Building Society); **www.chlmortgages.co.uk** (Capital Home Loans); **www.cheltglos.co.uk** (Cheltenham and Gloucester); **www.fnmc.co.uk** (First National Mortgage Company); **www.halifax.co.uk** (Halifax); **www.if.com** (Intelligent Finance); **www.kmc.co.uk** (Kensington Mortgage Company); **www.mortgageexpress.co.uk** (Mortgage Express); **www.nationwide.co.uk** (Nationwide Building Society); **www.northernrock.co.uk** (Northern Rock); **www.npbs.co.uk** (Norwich and Peterborough Building Society); **www.portman.co.uk** (Portman Building Society); **www.scottishbldgsoc.co.uk** (Scottish Building Society); **www.ucbhomeloans.co.uk** (UCB Home Loans); **www.virginone.co.uk** (Virgin); **www.woolwich.co.uk** (Woolwich); **www.ybs.co.uk** (Yorkshire Building Society).

For further information, the Council of Mortgage Lenders (C.M.L.) has factsheets on all aspects of homebuying. The Building Societies Association can provide contact details of all societies.

If things go wrong, The Financial Services Authority oversees financial services organisations and can deal with complaints about them, or contact the Banking and Building Societies Ombudsman.

INSURANCE TO PROTECT YOUR MORTGAGE PAYMENTS

Although the temptation when you've decided to buy a home is to rush round all the estate agents on day one, it really pays to know your financial position clearly from the start – and that includes the rather uninspiring subject of insurance.

Assistance for mortgage payers on state benefits has been reduced in recent years, increasing the need for insurance safeguards. For mortgages taken out since 1 October 1995 you get no help for the first nine months and then it is capped at £100,000. Therefore, according to the Council of Mortgage Lenders, more than a third of new borrowers take out mortgage payment protection insurance. Permanent Health Insurance and Critical Illness cover are alternatives. All are looked at below.

Be sure to check the small print of any policies you consider. Definitions and cover can vary greatly.

INSURANCE TYPES

LIFE INSURANCE   Life insurance is not essential if you live on your own and do not have any dependants. It is more important if you have a partner or a family. Life insurance does not have to be linked with the mortgage amount and term and can be increased in later years, although the younger and healthier you are, the cheaper it is.

TERM ASSURANCE

Term assurance or insurance is the cheapest and simplest type of life cover. It pays out the lump sum insured if you were to die within the specified period, for example 25 years. There is no investment element, so if you are alive after the specified term you receive no payment back. Policy cost depends on your age and state of health and the insurer may require you to undergo medical tests.

You can choose between a **level term policy** – where the amount insured never varies, and which is therefore suitable for an interest-only loan – and a **decreasing term policy** – where the amount you insure decreases each year. The latter is therefore suitable for a repayment mortgage as the total amount owed reduces each year. With both types your monthly premiums remain the same throughout the whole term of the insurance.

If you have an endowment mortgage, life insurance is built-in, but for other mortgage types you will have to add this cover separately. Your mortgage company may insist you take this type of cover out, but if anyone depends upon you financially – for example, if you have a family or you are buying with friends who rely on you paying your share of the mortgage – you should take it out anyway.

WHOLE-OF-LIFE INSURANCE

This is the other main type of life insurance, though far less common. Rather than covering a specified term, this lasts throughout your life and therefore guarantees your dependants a payout. It can more expensive than term assurance, although most policies are issued on a 'with-profits' basis, meaning that bonuses are added to the policy. Policies can be surrendered at any time.

With this type of insurance you may be able to increase the amount you have insured without the need for further medical tests, for example at marriage, the birth of a child or moving to a more expensive property.

LIFE INSURANCE FOR GAY BUYERS

When you apply for cover, life insurance companies may ask whether your partner is homosexual, following this up with a lifestyle questionnaire. Non-disclosure or providing false information invalidates the insurance and makes reapplying to other companies difficult. On completion of the form the insurance company may request a test to determine whether you are HIV positive or not. Simply taking the test can cause some insurers to decline cover, even if you test negative. Testing positive will make it difficult to buy life insurance.

If you feel that you have been treated unfairly by an insurance company, over this or any other issue, contact the Association of British Insurers.

CRITICAL ILLNESS INSURANCE

This has gained greatly in popularity in recent years. This pays out a lump sum for permanent total disability and if you are diagnosed with any of a range of specified serious medical conditions such as cancer, heart disease and stroke. Usually a list of conditions can be tailor-made for you, but there can be notable exclusions (for example, usually not all cancers are covered). Obviously, critical illness cover is more expensive than life cover, because you are about 2.5 times more likely to suffer a critical illness than die before the age of 65. It could therefore be seen as being more important than life insurance, especially if you are single. It is usually coupled with or added to the life insurance policy but can be a stand-alone policy.

MORTGAGE PAYMENT PROTECTION INSURANCE (M.P.P.I.)

Mortgage Payment Protection Insurance is worth considering although not essential. It will pay your mortgage for a set period if you cannot work because you have an illness or accident or become unemployed. Policies typically start paying one month after you are out of work for up to a year, so they are geared to short-term unemployment only. M.P.P.I. can be bought from a financial adviser or direct from the company as a stand-alone policy.

ACCIDENT, SICKNESS AND UNEMPLOYMENT INSURANCE (A.S.U.)

Accident, sickness and unemployment insurance is similar to M.P.P.I. but can be taken out to cover other financial products such as store and credit cards and loans. Most policies pay out when you have been out of work for a month.

INCOME PROTECTION INSURANCE

Also known as permanent health insurance (P.H.I.) or income replacement insurance, this pays you a monthly sum in the event of you not being able to work because of illness or disability. It generally pays out for non-life-threatening conditions like stress-related illness or back problems and cost depends upon age, sex and job, and when you want payments to start should you make a claim.

Payments continue until either you recover and return to work, until you die or reach the end of the policy term. The maximum you can insure is usually 60 per cent of your gross income. Some policies have a with-profits or unit-linked investment element, providing a lump sum on retirement.

This form of insurance is particularly suitable for the self-employed who do not qualify for employers' sickness benefit. If you have an employer, check to see if it provides a benefit package, which may be part of your pension provision. You should consider taking out income protection insurance if your employer does not provide any or adequate cover.

INSURANCE WEBSITES

Try **www.moneynet.co.uk**, **www.moneysupermarket.co.uk**, **www.lifepoliciesdirect.co.uk**, **www.rapidinsure.co.uk** and **www.ftyourmoney.co.uk** to find out more about the exciting world of insurance.

USEFUL TELEPHONE NUMBERS/EMAIL ADDRESSES

ENDOWMENT POLICIES AND GAY MEN

Massow Financial Services: 0800 328 0625

CREDIT REFERENCE AGENCIES

Experian: PO Box 8000, Nottingham NG1 5GX, 0115 976 8747; Equifax: PO Box 3001, Glasgow G81 2DT, 0990 143700 and Callcredit: PO Box 491, Leeds LS1 5XX.

REPOSSESSION

Consumer Credit Counselling Service: 0800 138 1111
National Debt Line: 0808 808 4000
Payplan: 0800 0845 298

7 FINDING A HOME

THE SEARCH FOR YOUR DREAM HOME

Having decided the type of property you are after and how much you can afford, you are ready to begin the search for your ideal home.

To give an idea of the stages the typical property purchase goes through, here is a <u>buyer's timetable</u>:

- You decide what kind of property you want to buy and its approximate price and location
- You select a mortgage and obtain an offer in principle
- You begin your search, registering with agents, surfing the net and so on
- You find a solicitor who will act for you
- Having found a property, you make an offer, usually through an agent
- If your offer is accepted, the property should be taken off the market
- You instruct your solicitor to start the conveyancing process
- Your solicitor requests the title deeds to the property from the vendor's solicitor or establishes ownership through the Land Registry and contract negotiations begin
- Your mortgage lender requires a valuation of the property
- You also have a survey done if required
- Your mortgage lender receives the valuation and agrees to lend the money
- Your solicitor makes various checks concerning the property including a local authority search
- You negotiate on fixtures and fittings and any problems the survey may have highlighted, if required
- Your solicitor finalises contract and mortgage details
- You pay the deposit for the property to your solicitor
- Contracts are exchanged and the completion date agreed
- Your solicitor draws up the transfer deed, signed by buyer and seller
- Your mortgage lender pays the loan into your solicitor's account, which is transferred to the vendor's solicitor on the completion date and your solicitor receives the keys to the property, the transfer deed and Land Registry certificate
- Your solicitor pays the stamp duty and forwards the transfer deed to the Land Registry so that you are registered as the new owner
- Your solicitor forwards the title deed or Land Registry certificate from the Land Registry to your mortgage lender as security for the loan

BEGINNING THE SEARCH

Although the majority of homes are bought and sold through estate agents, there are a number of alternative ways and this chapter will examine the options.

ESTATE AGENTS

To start with, register your details with the estate agents (and in Scotland, also with lawyers' property centres) in the area where you wish to buy, in person if possible. In areas that have plenty of agents, concentrate on those that deal largely with the type of home you're after. Cowboys are relatively rare these days, but before dealing with an agent check that they belong to a professional body such as the National Association of Estate Agents, which has a Code of Practice to adhere to and an indemnity fund for cases of fraud, or contact the Ombudsman for Estate Agents.

In a busy market, buyers in the strongest position are the ones tipped off early about new properties coming on to the market. Such buyers contact the agent regularly, are accessible, and ready to swoop if the right property appears, with the money in place and, if they are selling, their home already on the market.

Make it as easy as possible for the agent to contact you – giving your mobile number and email address, and a fax number for receiving property details, for example.

Be specific about what you are and are not looking for and even so, examine the property particulars you receive carefully before viewing as some agents can be notorious for sending out details for properties that are entirely unsuitable.

Even though you have registered your interest it is important to regularly check the agent's website and telephone or call in to see if new properties have come on to the agent's books. Note the names of the agents you deal with as you are more likely to be informed of the latest suitable properties on the market if you are on first-name terms. When a property becomes available, ask questions on the phone to lessen the chance of seeing something unsuitable.

Tell the agent if you have finance arranged or if you are not in a 'chain' (that is, you are not dependent upon your buyers having to sell and their buyers having to sell and so on). An agent will look upon these situations favourably.

Try to reserve a weekday for house-hunting as agents will be less busy than at weekends and often vendors will be more approachable as their leisure time isn't invaded. On weekdays you'll have more chance of the agent being able to ferry you to properties, feeding you extra info on the area as he does so. Make notes about each property so that it's not all a blur at the end of the day.

Because in the past there was an unacceptable degree of inaccuracy, exaggerating or plain lying about properties some agents sold, the Property Misdescriptions Act was brought in. But problems still occur, especially as most agents' details carry a disclaimer, so it is important to check the accuracy of the property particulars yourself.

If you're looking for a property and it is on with more than one agent, it's a good idea to compare their particulars as they can be surprisingly different.

THE INTERNET

This is an increasingly popular way of searching for a home although websites vary greatly in quality. A good site can save a lot of time but there are those that have few properties, many still appearing on the site despite having sold months ago.

Some have a regional bias or charge for buying or selling. There may be an email facility that contacts you when an appropriate property becomes available. As well as offering properties for sale in the UK, some sites also offer properties to rent or for sale abroad. Tips on homebuying and other services and features are common.

Many agents and housebuilders operate their own websites but much more useful are the property portals that contain hundreds or thousands of properties offered by a number of agents as well as, sometimes, private sales too.

PROPERTY WEBSITES

The biggest, with good nationwide coverage, are:
www.fish4homes.co.uk (with about 250,000 homes available at any time); **www.rightmove.co.uk** (160,000 homes);
www.assertahome.com (150,000 homes);
www.primelocation.com (40,000 homes);
www.propertyfinder.co.uk (38,000 homes).

Other sites include:
www.ukpropertyshop.com; **www.homepages.co.uk**;
www.homemovers.co.uk; **www.smartestates.com**;

www.housesearch.uk.com; www.estateagent.co.uk;
www.hol365.com; www.home-sale.co.uk; www.linkprop.co.uk;
www.homedirectory.com; www.pattinson.co.uk;
www.housenet.co.uk; www.houseweb.co.uk; www.homes-on-
line.co.uk; www.home-to-home.co.uk; www.movewithus.co.uk;
www.numberone4property.co.uk; www.propertyshowroom.com;
www.homedirectory.com; www.findaproperty.com;
www.purehomes.com; www.reallymoving.com;
www.propertylive.co.uk; www.home.co.uk;
www.nethomes.uk.com.

Some sites enable vendors to advertise their properties for free
or at little cost, avoiding the need to go through an estate agent.
These include:
www.ukpropertysales.com; www.loot.com;
www.propertybroker.co.uk; www.4salebyowner.co.uk;
www.easier.co.uk; www.thelittlehousecompany.co.uk;
www.houseweb.co.uk; www.homeownersales.co.uk;
www.homesalez.com; www.homefreehome.co.uk.

Note that the Property Misdescriptions Act, which prevents estate
agents from exaggerating the virtues of properties they are selling,
does not cover private sales or private sales sites.

CHECKING OUT THE NEIGHBOURHOOD AND OTHER INFORMATION

As well as getting a good feel for the local property market you are
focusing upon, you can glean an amazing amount of information
including potential environmental risks, school league tables, noise
levels, entertainment venues and neighbourhood home pages from
some sites.

www.homecheck.co.uk, for example, gives instant access to a
range of information concerning environmental risks not revealed
on traditional building surveys or local authority searches.
Information available includes contamination from old industrial
sites, landfill sites, radon gas, subsidence and flooding as well as
detailed information about your neighbourhood.

www.environment-agency.gov.uk, a government website, offers
information on local matters like flooding and pollution.

www.upmystreet.com includes statistics and details on house
prices, schools, colleges, shops, services, unemployment, council
tax, crime and even ambulance response times for localities.

www.home-envirosearch.com reveals environmental factors connected with your home.

www.homesight.co.uk, run by credit reference agency Equifax and Yellow Pages, can provide free brief reports and or detailed ones for £86.

Point a web browser at **www.multimap.com**, type in the postcode, town or street name, and you'll get maps, homes for sale and to rent, entertainment venues, neighbourhood home pages, pubs, clubs and businesses.

Key in the Friends of the Earth website, **www.foe.co.uk**, to see if there are companies nearby that it claims are polluting the area.

The National Air Quality Information Archive (**www.airquality.co.uk**) provides general air pollution information.

The Landmark Information Group (**www.landmark-information.co.uk**) can provide further environmental information specific to your chosen area.

www.homemovers.co.uk, as well as having over 200,000 properties for sale, also contains details like typical house prices, buying trends, risks from subsidence, local amenities, car crime and burglary rates for a locality.

The Land Registry website, **www.landreg.gov.uk**, has lots of information on property prices in general and the price paid for any house or flat sold in England or Wales since April 2000 is available for a fee of £4. A similar scheme is operated by the Land Registry In Scotland.

These sites also contain information about various aspects of searching for a home, such as conveyancing, surveying, removals and finding a builder: **www.pattinson.co.uk**; **www.ihavemoved.com**; **www08004homes.com**; **www.HomePro.com**; **www.freehomeindex.com**; **www.Home2Home.co.uk**; **www.underoneroof.co.uk**; **www.homefile.co.uk**; **www.homesight.co.uk**; **www.county-homesearch.co.uk**.

www.smartestates.com can help in the search for mortgages, surveying, conveyancing and removals, and has a change of address service.

www.reallymoving.com offers online quotes from surveyors, solicitors, removal companies, and insurance and cleaning services. It even has an email reminder service that contacts you as and when things need organising.

PROFESSIONAL PROPERTY FINDERS

Property search agents can save a buyer a lot of time. Say you work from eight to eight, you're only going to be able to view on a Saturday along with everyone else. And if an estate agent says on

Monday he's got a property and you can't see it until Saturday, in a heated market the likelihood is that it will be gone by then. You need someone to source, check out and weed out the properties.

Many buyers do not consider using a property search company, or buying agent, because they assume the cost would be too great. But often this option can *save* money. It also saves time, banishing the need to wade through piles of property particulars and to drive miles to view a house that looked great on paper, but in reality is not suitable.

Buying agents, because they are an impartial third party, can be more successful at negotiating a lower purchase price or rental terms than the purchaser, whose keenness to acquire the property can mean he's not level-headed during the bargaining process.

The saving can far exceed the cost of using a property search agent, whose charges are typically a registration fee of around £300 plus 1.5 per cent of the purchase price (or 15 per cent of the saving between the asking and purchase price, whichever is greater).

A property search agent can offer other advantages. Knowing the locality well, he can point out potential but less obvious pitfalls such as a proposed bypass or a nearby flight path. And he will probably ask many more questions about the move than the buyer may have asked himself. He will also provide information about things like local schools, council offices, shops and transport, and usually will not charge extra for this. He will provide local maps and can transfer utilities in the buyers' name. He can put clients in touch with solicitors, removal firms, surveyors, builders and other professionals.

A good agent will talk at length to the client to see how flexible they can be. Often this will reveal problems like large furniture that has to be accommodated, or that a train station has to be nearby if the buyer is going to get visitors.

Buying agents often find potential in a property even though it may not match the checklist exactly. If a large house is required to also accommodate an office, for example, the agent may suggest a smaller, cheaper building with a barn attached that could be converted to make up the extra space.

Because property search companies are constantly in touch with local estate agents and property experts, they have good knowledge of the area's market trends, current prices and how much similar properties have recently sold for. They often know of an owner's intention to sell or rent before the property is placed on the market. They are able to find properties that are not generally available, such as those being sold discreetly without active marketing.

But enlisting the help of a search company isn't suitable for all property sales. It would usually be uneconomic for them to help find a property worth under about £80,000.

A list of relocation agents is available from the Association of Relocation Agents.

Other ways to search for a home:

PROPERTY PAGES IN THE PRESS

As well as looking out for 'For Sale' boards, regularly read the property pages of the local papers, although the time lapse between placing the ad and it appearing can mean the property you want to see may already be under offer in a busy seller's market. You can also place advertisements on these pages indicating the sort of property you are looking for.

LEAFLETING

You could post leaflets through doors in your chosen streets saying what you are looking for. Mention that you are a private individual rather than an agent after more business. Leafleting may seem like a long shot, but people tend to move home every six to eight years or so and therefore a road with a hundred houses is likely to have more than one coming up for sale each month. Buying a property this way avoids an estate agent's fee, and can mean a saving for both parties.

RELOCATING

If you are moving to a different area some distance away the area will probably be new to you and opportunities for viewings probably infrequent. Consider selling or letting out your present property and renting in the new area for a while so you get your bearings and have a much better idea of where you want to live and how much you want to pay.

VIEWING

If a property looks pig ugly from the photo, persevere. Appearances are deceptive, and you can be pleasantly surprised. Don't just look at the cosmetics of the house – think what you can do with it.

You need to have a flexible approach, as you are never going to find the perfect house. If you want a detached home, don't rule out a terraced one, for example.

Saying that, it is easy to be seduced by a property where you're so keen to move in you overlook the disadvantages that could become a real headache later on. To ensure that this doesn't happen, take a notebook and tape measure and work through a checklist of things to look out for from the very first viewing. Make plenty of notes as you go round, especially if you are looking at other properties in the day as you can soon get confused about what feature you saw where.

Don't allow yourself to be rushed by the seller or estate agent. Ask them lots of questions. How long has the property been on the market? Has anyone else made an offer and why did it not proceed? If the seller bought recently or a previous buyer dropped out, is a survey available? How ready and able is the seller to move? Is he in a chain? Are copies of bills showing running costs available? Are there guarantees for work done such as damp-proofing? What are the annual costs, such as water, heating, council tax? What are the neighbours like?

LEASEHOLD PROPERTIES

If the property is leasehold it's a good idea to ask for copies of the service charge demands for the last few years. What is the length of the lease and the ground rent charge, and are there maintenance or service charges? Blocks of flats often have service charges, which can be surprisingly hefty. Are there any restrictions, such as a ban on pets? Have the charges risen sharply, or have there been a high number of costly repairs? Are the managing agents efficient? It's good to try to speak to other leaseholders to see their point of view too.

OUTSIDE

Although it's easy to change the wallpaper or the fitted kitchen you won't be able to change the position of the property, its views and the light it receives so focus on these closely.

East-facing rooms are sunnier in the morning while west-facing ones get more light in the afternoon. Are there trees nearby that could block out light at a different time of year? If the approach to the property is steep, will access be a problem in icy conditions? If industry or a farm is nearby, would noise or smoke be a problem?

A nearby river or stream could pose a threat of flooding, and if the property is near the coast there could also be the problem of coastal erosion. Such factors could affect insurance cover.

INSIDE

If the property clearly satisfies at least your minimum requirements at first viewing, look again in more detail. Will the layout allow you adequate space for your needs? Is there adequate space for large items of furniture? Can they be brought into the room you plan them for? You don't want to have to pay for a crane or a hoist or for removing a window to install your beloved sofa into the sitting room. Measure large items first and check with a tape measure at the property.

What kind of heating is used? Does it look like it may need updating? If there is an electric cooker, is mains gas available? Do the electrics look modern and are there enough power points or does it look like you would have to consider rewiring – a costly and messy job. Is noise a problem? Open a window to hear the traffic noise.

In the hall, is there space for a pushchair or bicycle, for coats, wellington boots and umbrellas? Is the dining area or dining room convenient for the kitchen? Is the layout of the kitchen suitable for your needs or easy to change? Is there space for your appliances, and where would a washing machine go? Is the staircase suitable for the very young or elderly?

If it is an older property, has it been modernised well? Have period features like coving and sash windows been retained? Maybe some features, such as fireplaces, have been covered up.

If buying semi-detached or terraced, what is the condition of the properties next door? If your neighbour uses their front garden as a rubbish tip, it will hardly cause buyers to flock to your door should you ever wish to sell. If their roof is in a bad condition this could possibly cause problems with damp in your home too.

Is there wall cavity insulation? Are the boiler and pipes lagged or insulated? If there are any lead pipes these should be replaced. Visit the loft to see whether the roof is insulated. If the light is turned off there should not be any patches of daylight. Do the timbers show any signs of vermin, damp or woodworm?

Don't worry overly if the way the property is decorated differs significantly from how you would do things. The bulk of what you're usually paying for with property comes down to location and cosmetic things can usually be easily and inexpensively changed.

STRUCTURAL PROBLEMS

Before shelling out on a survey you can get a good idea of the condition of a property just by looking out for certain indicators.

Be wary of new wallpaper or paint, which could be concealing cracks or damp patches.

Cracks around doors and bay windows and long diagonal cracks across walls which look like they have been repaired but have again cracked could indicate subsidence where the foundations of the property are not secure and which can be very costly to rectify. Are doors sticking or not hanging correctly? A sloping floor, bent chimney stack or uneven roof line can indicate subsidence.

The messy job of underpinning a small detached house because of subsidence will cost from around £20,000. Obtaining buildings insurance can be problematic and costly, but the Subsidence Claims Advisory Bureau and the Insurance Ombudsman Bureau may be able to offer advice in such cases. For more details contact the Association of Specialist Underpinning Contractors.

Cracked or sagging plaster ceilings in older houses can be an often underestimated danger and messy to repair.

Springy floors can be a sign that the floors themselves or joists underneath may have woodworm.

A musty smell and cracking in woodwork can indicate dry rot, caused by a fungus (*serpula lacrynens*), which is usually very expensive to treat, especially as all the affected wood, down to window frames and joists, must be replaced. Many buyers wouldn't dream of buying a house with dry rot unless they can negotiate a hefty discount off the asking price, love the house and don't mind considerable mess and disruption.

Bulging outside walls can be a sign of subsidence. To see if a wall is bulging, stand close to the end of it and look along it to see whether it is straight.

Nearby trees may have roots that could undermine the property's foundations.

The damp-proof course: is it above the soil? If it isn't there could be potential problems. Older properties won't necessarily have a damp-proof course, which can cause damp on the ground floor.

Stains on ceilings and walls can indicate damp, although this may be less serious than it looks, perhaps penetrative damp caused by a leaking roof, window or gutter, which should go away once the culprit is fixed. Is there a smell of damp? Can you feel moisture on walls? More serious is *rising damp*, when a damp-proof course breaks down and the brick walls suck up water from the ground. Typically in this situation you will have wet walls with damp, discoloured wallpaper on the lower portion of the walls, possibly a smell of mouldy paper, flaking paintwork and crumbling plaster. If you are not sure of the cause of the damp, contact the British Wood Preserving and Damp-proofing Association to find a local experienced damp consultant.

Roof tiles and slates: move some way from the house to have a look at the condition. Even better, use binoculars. Do the chimney stacks look in good condition?

Pointing: examine this (the mortar between the bricks) because if it is in a bad condition it can allow damp into the property.

Loft/attic: the existence of stains could indicate a damaged roof. Is the loft insulated? Is it big enough for the possibility that it could be converted into living space? There is no guarantee that this would be permitted but is more likely if neighouring properties have conversions.

Cellar: Are there signs of dry rot in the form of a flat fungus growth? Dry rot is costly to eradicate. Does the cellar seem damp? You may even be able to see moisture on the walls.

THE NEIGHBOURHOOD

Are there shops and public transport within easy walking distance? What are nearby properties like? If the one you want to buy is in good condition but others in the road are in bad repair, it could bring down the value of yours.

Visit again at different times of day and look for possible causes of disturbance in the locality. A seemingly quiet pub nearby may spring to life and create disturbance in the evening, a school may cause lots of noise and traffic problems at drop-off and pick-up times and a newsagent may get daily deliveries of papers in the early hours.

THE BUYING PROCESS

PLAN AHEAD

Ideally, soon after you start to look for properties you want to look into selecting the solicitor who will do your conveyancing so that you will be ready to go when the right property comes up.

ENGAGING A SOLICITOR

You will need to appoint a solicitor to do the conveyancing once your offer to buy has been agreed, but the sooner you find one the better. They will check that the seller is the property's rightful owner, look into potential problems like rights of way or major developments planned in the locality that could affect the property, and, if you are buying a flat, check the lease. Your solicitor will oversee the transfer of funds to complete the sale and register the change of ownership with the Land Registry.

The legal process can be slow, and hold ups can lose you the property, so choose your solicitor with care. Choose one that specialises in conveyancing. Their fees can vary incredibly widely (a recent Consumers' Association survey found conveyancing costs on one house ranging from £120 to £750) as well as their expertise and enthusiasm.

If you can't get one through personal recommendation, consult the Yellow Pages and get quotes and opinions from several before making a final choice. Ask whether you will be charged a fixed fee, and, if so, ask whether this includes everything, down to the search and electronic bank transfer fees, postage and VAT. Ask what the charges will be if the sale falls through.

Similarly, if you get a guide price you could be charged for every fax or letter on top.

When you include extras like a local authority search (£50–£150), the Land Registry fee (around £100–£200) and bank telegraphic transfer of mortgage money fees (around £30–£40), as well as stamp duty if the price is above £60,000, it is not unusual to pay over £600 + VAT for a modest property.

Generally, the bigger the property and better the location, the more you pay, especially if there are any legal problems related to the sale. If you're buying in London or any other expensive city, non-metropolitan solicitors can be significantly cheaper and as it does not matter where the solicitor is located, you can save money by using one in the sticks.

After you have made the offer on the property you want, badger your solicitor regularly to make sure your file stays at the top of their invariably large pile of clients.

If you have a complaint to make about your solicitor, contact the Office for the Supervision of Solicitors.

DIY CONVEYANCING

It is possible to do your own conveyancing but this can be complicated for the layman and could be a false economy as a mistake can be expensive to put right.

Obviously, the more straightforward the move, the simpler the legal process. Therefore, going the DIY route is more suitable if you're buying with cash rather than taking out a mortgage, and purchasing the freehold rather than a lease. Similarly, it is probably unwise to tackle the job if the property is not registered, is in Scotland, is part of a property, is sold at auction, is being sold by a divorcing or separating couple, is being sold new by a builder or developer, or is not wholly occupied by the seller.

If you were to do your own conveyancing, as a purchaser you would have to check that the other person has the right to sell the property and that the title to the property is effective. The deposit can be paid by cheque into the vendor's solicitor's bank account.

You would need to check that there are no potential problems such as a motorway planned for the end of your garden. Solicitors do this by checking whether any planning applications have been submitted, but informal research such as surfing the net, talking to neighbours and planning officers and reading local papers can glean more relevant information. Solicitors conduct an environmental search but checking a website like **www.homecheck.co.uk** can unearth lots of facts.

When such preliminaries are satisfied you would have to check the draft contract, send out forms about the property for the vendor to fill in, exchange contracts, complete, pay the stamp duty, forward forms to the Land Registry and transfer the funds to the vendor. This is generally done by electronic transfer, which you can ask your bank to do.

You would need to buy a set of standard forms for searches, the Land Registry and enquiries of the vendor. These are available from the Land Registry and Oyez (**www.oyez.co.uk**).

LICENSED CONVEYANCERS

If your mortgage lender does not object, you can use a licensed conveyancer (or qualified conveyancer in Scotland) rather than a fully fledged lawyer, but make sure their credentials are valid. This option may be cheaper.

Further details, and a list of licensed conveyancers in your area, are available from the Council for Licensed Conveyancers and the Society of Licensed Conveyancers. In Scotland contact the Scottish Conveyancing and Executry Services Board.

For a list of solicitors in your area (and of solicitors who can take on claims against solicitors who have been negligent in handling the purchase of your property), contact the Law Society, the Law Society of Scotland, the Law Society of Northern Ireland or the National Solicitors' Network.

ONLINE CONVEYANCING

A growing number of legal websites offer the services of conveyancing solicitors, where everything is done by email or by text messages from your mobile phone and advice and application forms can be downloaded.

Bear in mind that an Internet lawyer may be cheaper than a conventional one but not necessarily, and you would be unlikely to be able to pick up the telephone and get an instant answer to a query.

The price charged usually relates to the purchase price. For example, at the time of going to press, Easier2Move (**www.easier2move.co.uk**) charges £325 for the purchase or sale of a property worth up to £100,000, with remortgages coming in at £199. VAT and disbursements (such as search fees) are extra, as with a normal solicitor's service.

Many on-line conveyancers operate a 'no completion, no fee' service so that if the sale is scuppered by gazumping, for example, the fees are waived.

CONVEYANCING WEBSITES

www.assertahome.com; www.pattinson.co.uk;
www.e-zeemoves.com; www.movingahead.co.uk;
www.perfectlylegal.co.uk; www.onlineconveyancing.co.uk;
www.conveyancingnationwide.co.uk;
www.conveyancingonline.com; www.smartestates.com;
www.conveyancing24-7.com.

WHEN YOU HAVE FOUND A PROPERTY: MAKING AN OFFER

BEFORE MAKING THE OFFER

Finding the property you want is often a formidable task in itself, but the next substantial hurdle can be actually clinching the deal.

Before making an offer, visit the property again at different times to ensure it is the property for you. Find out when the vendor is likely to be in a position to move. A lengthy chain could cause considerable hold-ups. Would the property be so attractive then?

Ascertain exactly what will remain and what will be removed from the property. The final contract drawn up by the seller's solicitor will list such items but the more you know beforehand the better equipped you are for making an offer.

Ask whether items like curtains, curtain rails and tracks, carpets and built-in cookers can be included in the price or bought cheaply.

They may not suit the seller's new home or be too much trouble to move. What about lampshades, wall lights, built-in cupboards, shelving, garden furniture and plants, and sheds. Would you be interested in buying the refrigerator, dishwasher, washing machine, tumble dryer and other such appliances?

You've got to sell yourself to your seller, so be friendly and don't discuss how you're going to transform their disgusting hovel into your dream home in front of them. Try to establish any mutual interests, such as a love of golf or having children at the same school.

If you want to make an offer, don't waste everyone's time, possibly permanently destroying your chances of being taken seriously, by offering far less than the price being asked unless you know the vendor is desperate to sell. Don't be vague but show your enthusiasm for the property and that you're serious about buying. Confirm your offer with a handwritten letter. Knock on the door and initiate a chat where the agent is not in the background.

IS THE PROPERTY BEING OFFERED AT A FAIR PRICE?

There are so many factors that can affect the value of a home. Proximity to water, seclusion, mature gardens and selling in the summer all help to increase the value of a property, as do easy access to main commuting routes, being well sited in an attractive village or town (such as near a park, on the village green or on the edge of a village).

Factors like noise from a flight path, motorway or railway line, a nearby nightclub, restaurant, tower block, council or industrial estate, or electricity pylon are among the many things that can hinder a property's value. A property in an unattractive location or a large property with inadequate land won't do much to boost a homeowner's coffers.

A noisy, rough school nearby could hinder a sale while a property in the catchment area of a good one could do wonders to the asking price. South-facing is better than north-facing for the added sunlight.

A greater number of bedrooms does not necessarily mean a greater price. Restructuring a house to reduce the five bedrooms to three, if done well, could enhance profitability as the resulting light, spacious design with maybe a gallery and other novel features can be especially appealing.

The best price for a property is achieved when its location does not suffer any negative aspects, and has attractive outlooks from all windows. Even if you do not have this, you can still enhance saleability by ensuring the home is uncluttered inside and immaculately decorated in neutral tones and paperwork confirms improvements like damp-proofing, rewiring and a relatively new central heating system.

Added space, such as an extension, should be in keeping with the house. The exterior should have been relatively recently painted.

The asking price will go down if sash windows have been replaced with modern aluminium ones, a slate is missing from the roof, or there's a few suspect cracks in the walls which could suggest serious structural problems.

It's easy to spend a fortune on a property, but if the seller has spent it on the wrong things, the value of the property could plummet. Ill-thought-out fake period features like Victorian lamps, a satellite dish, stone cladding, a badly designed extension, loud carpets, a fondness for strong dark paint and violently patterned wallpapers, a clutter of furniture, a garden cramming in flamboyant ornaments and too many features like a pond, rockery and patio can all cause values to reduce.

MAKING THE OFFER

Vendors usually realise that their property may sell for under the 'asking price'. Offer the asking price only if the property is your absolute dream home, you know the seller won't accept a lower offer, there are lots of people chasing similar properties, or you are sure it is a bargain.

It is a good idea to offer a bit less than the maximum amount you are prepared to pay. So, if the property has an asking price of £100,000 and you would be happy to pay £97,000, try offering around £94,000 first.

Establish how long the property has been on the market. The longer it is, the more likely the vendor will be receptive to bargaining.

When you are making a lower offer, point out problems that could be expensive to put right, such as ancient wiring and missing roof slates.

Sell your advantages as a buyer. If you are not involved in a chain, say so.

When you are confident of the price you wish to offer, if the seller is using an estate agent, put it to them. Don't say that you would be prepared to offer more if it is refused – remember, the agent is acting for the seller.

You may have to wait for a decision, your offer may be accepted or rejected straight away, or you may then enter a period of haggling. Don't hold things up for the sake of a few hundred pounds. In many areas, where prices are rising steadily, it is important to move fast to make the sale go through. If it fails because you quibbled over £500 it could cost you far more once you've had to start the homebuying process all over again.

IF YOUR OFFER IS ACCEPTED

Even if it is accepted, in England and Wales your offer is only 'subject to contract and survey' and therefore if you change your mind about buying – maybe because the survey shows up unforeseen problems, there are hitches with the mortgage, the local search finds that a superstore is about to be built at the end of the garden, or you just go off the idea – you can walk away from the deal without penalty.

When it is accepted, inform your solicitor and lender. Request that *all* estate agents handling the property are informed that it is no longer on the market.

To avoid gazumping (being outbid by another buyer), try to get your vendor to agree to a legally binding lockout clause, which your solicitor can arrange, where they promise not to consider other offers for a stated period, say two weeks. This gives you time to progress the sale.

Organise a survey as quickly as possible as it shows your commitment. It turns it into a moral, though not legally binding, obligation for the seller to sell to you.

Before a lender will loan you the money to buy the property it will carry out a valuation and there is a possibility that it will value the property at below the offer price. This can sometimes work in your favour and help you to negotiate a lower price, but, unless you have other means to raise the shortfall, it could mean you lose the property to someone able to pay the asking price.

CONTRACT RACE

Unless you are desperate for the property, be very wary of entering into a 'contract race' where two or more potential buyers are told by the vendor that the first buyer able to exchange contracts can have the property. Contract races are most likely when there is a shortage of properties or the seller wants to move quickly. You could spend considerable sums in surveying and search and legal fees only to lose the property. Even if you win the race, the seller is not legally obliged to sell to you and can still opt for someone else.

SURVEYS

SELLERS' PACKS

By 2006, the government plans to introduce sellers' packs, an initiative that will make it compulsory for sellers of property to commission a survey of their property as well as provide various other documents (such as an energy efficiency assessment, a draft contract, title documents, local authority searches, planning and building regulation approvals, warranties and guarantees on work carried out) to speed up homebuying and therefore eliminate gazumping. The packs will typically cost sellers in excess of £500. Until such a legal requirement comes in, it is still very highly recommended that prospective buyers seriously consider commissioning a survey of most types of property they wish to buy.

WHY SHOULD YOU GET A SURVEY DONE?

Some homebuyers swear that surveys are the best few hundred pounds you can spend, and can save you from buying a home full of potential disaster, while others say that you're paying through the nose for a jumped up overpriced professional to tell you the obvious, like where the light switches are or that the hall could do with a repaint, and if he makes a mistake he can hide behind the small print. Which opinion is right?

Well, certainly surveyors sometimes miss serious defects in properties they examine, but as buying a home is likely to be your biggest purchase, in most cases (though not usually if you are buying a newly built home covered by a good warranty, for example) it seems to make sense to have it looked at by an expert.

A lender's valuation, despite costing around £100–£200, is extremely brief and is designed simply to assure the lender that the property is worth as much or more than the amount they are lending. A homebuyer's survey or full structural survey may cost considerably more, but it can save far more by revealing unseen horrors and suggesting ways to deal with them. And there is usually comeback if the surveyor gets it wrong.

When you're buying a house it is easy to become emotionally attached while a surveyor can look at the property dispassionately. You end up knowing what you're getting into and have a report that's extremely useful about what needs to be done to the property. If you send a copy to your insurers they can't come back to you later saying you didn't tell them about some aspect of the building. But you've got to be aware that there are things that will be excluded from the survey, and surveyors cannot examine everything, and cannot start ripping up carpets and floorboards.

Chartered surveyors can be recognised by the initials A.R.I.C.S. or F.R.I.C.S. after their names. The Royal Institution of Chartered Surveyors (R.I.C.S.) or, in Scotland, the Royal Institution of Chartered Surveyors in Scotland can provide names of members in your area. Alternatively, ask your lender's surveyor to carry out a survey on your behalf at the same time as the mortgage valuation, which should reduce costs.

Undeniably it is no fun being £500 out of pocket having had a comprehensive survey done if the house sale subsequently falls through, but it is better than buying and then finding unexpectedly that the property requires a new roof or has subsidence and needs underpinning. If you do pull out of a sale you may be able to recoup all or part of the survey's cost by transferring it to a subsequent buyer. Most vendors are happy to pass on your name to the new buyer to speed up the sale.

If a survey reveals problems, you have strong grounds for renegotiation on the price of the property. If you know serious defects would put you off the property you can ask the surveyor to telephone you the moment he finds any to save him writing the report and to save you having to pay his full fee.

When you're choosing a surveyor it's worth asking lots of questions about the extent of the inspection. You don't want a report full of trivia and stock phrases such as 'requires further investigation' or 'seek further specialist advice', although surveyors have to insert some caveats for fear of litigation. You have to accept that the report can't cover every eventuality, will have exclusion clauses, and may comment on things like wiring, plumbing, heating and so on, but the surveyor won't have necessarily gone as far as to test these.

Ask whether the surveyor is going to lift the floorboards, test the plumbing or move the wardrobes. Talk to several and find one you feel comfortable with. When obtaining quotes, ask each surveyor to detail exactly what will and will not be covered in the survey, so that you know exactly what you are paying for.

Ask whether the survey comes with a guarantee covering defects a surveyor should have seen but has missed. Will the survey be written in plain English which the average person can easily understand? Is the surveying firm based locally, and therefore knowledgeable about house prices and other considerations specific to the area? Does the company have a published complaints procedure?

SURVEY TYPES

THE VALUATION   These are not detailed structural surveys and as they are designed to simply find out whether the property is secure enough for the lender to feel happy about approving a mortgage secured on the property, serious structural problems may be spotted, but if they don't affect the lender, they may not appear on the report even if they could cause serious problems for you. Without knowing the potential defects of the property you could be unwittingly exposing yourself to crippling repair bills in the future. Sometimes the cost of the valuation is included as part of the package.

THE HOMEBUYER'S REPORT AND VALUATION   This is less thorough than a full survey and is intended for conventional houses, flats and bungalows and apparently in reasonable condition. Costing around £250–£450 (the older the property, the costlier it will be), it should report on the general condition of the property and point out significant defects that could affect the property's value as well as significant problems requiring inspection by a specialist, such as electrical faults. The surveyor should also look for problems like woodworm, wood rot and damp, and check drainage, insulation and damp-proofing. The market value of the property should be included, as well as rebuilding costs, which will be needed for buildings insurance purposes. But the surveyor is not obliged to move furniture, lift carpets, climb on to the roof to inspect tiles or reach other difficult or inaccessible areas, so important defects may be missed.

FULL STRUCTURAL SURVEY   The surveyor should look for structural defects, damp, dry and wet rot and check everything you ask for such as under the floorboards and on the roof. It's especially beneficial to have a full structural (or building) survey done if the property was built before around 1900, is in need of renovation, is listed or appears to have been significantly altered over the years. Many old buildings have been modernised to very varied standards which could cause structural problems. Some people commission a homebuyer's report and upgrade to a full survey if serious problems are suspected.

Full surveys can vary greatly in length and format, but, according to R.I.C.S., should provide a full picture of the property's construction and condition. It should contain extensive technical information on construction and materials as well as details of the whole range of defects. A valuation isn't necessarily provided and may cost extra.

All defects, major or minor, should be noted as well as the possible cost of repairs. There should be technical information about the construction of the building, its location and recommendations for further inspections required.

Full surveys vary in price considerably depending upon the surveyor, location, level of detail required and type of property but typically cost between £450 and £650 or over.

TAILORING YOUR SURVEY

Surveys can be tailored to your individual requirements. If, for example, you're an electrician and don't want to pay for details concerning the state of the wiring, this can be left out.

IF IT GOES WRONG

If you're unhappy with your survey, the R.I.C.S., whose members carry out the majority of surveys, has an arbitration scheme for claims against its members up to £50,000 which can be much cheaper and quicker than going to court, although there have been concerns that simply registering the complaint costs £250 upwards. The scheme is independently administered by the Chartered Institute of Arbitrators. Contact your solicitor for claims of a higher amount, which would require legal action.

COPING UNTIL COMPLETION

AFTER YOU HAVE RECEIVED THE SURVEY

If the survey throws up substantial problems that you were not expecting, try to renegotiate the price.

One of the many things the survey may reveal is that planning permission was not granted for work done on the home, such as an extension or conservatory. In this situation you can apply for retrospective planning permission from the local authority, costing around £100, but the process could delay the purchase by several months. If planning permission is not granted, in extreme circumstances the local authority can insist that the structure is demolished.

Between the offer 'subject to contract' being made and exchange of contracts, the seller's solicitor will ask the seller to complete a property information form, which asks whether there are any disputes or complaints involving neighbours. It is important to be truthful as you can be liable to pay damages if you answer untruthfully and this later comes to light.

One problem that can come up before exchange of contracts, where both sides sign a contract agreeing what is being bought and sold, is arguments over exactly what constitutes fixtures and fittings. There can be disagreements over what will be the completion date and sometimes renting temporarily or taking out a bridging loan may be the only way to stop the chain collapsing and save the deal.

When such problems are rectified or if the survey revealed no serious problems, you will be asked to lodge the deposit for the property with your solicitor and sign the contract. Only when 'exchange of contracts' takes place between your and the seller's solicitor are you legally bound to buy, while at the same time the vendor is legally committed to sell. Until then you are at risk of being gazumped.

GAZUMPING

Until exchange of contracts a buyer can be subjected to gazumping, where the seller, having accepted the buyer's offer, then decides to accept a higher offer from someone else. This can happen at any time before contracts are exchanged, because until the papers are signed there is no legal obligation to either buy or sell. Not only does the first buyer stand to lose the property, but they can also lose a substantial sum of money if surveys, searches and fees have been incurred.

By law the seller's agent is obliged to inform them of any offers made on their property, and it is up to the seller whether or not to reject them. If the vendor wants the property to be removed from the agent's register, he must request this in writing, and may not want to until the contracts are signed.

Fortunately, gazumping is relatively rare, whatever the newspaper headlines may sometimes suggest. To cut the chances of it happening move quickly (have your mortgage arranged and solicitor and surveyor ready the moment you make your offer), avoid haggling, and consider taking out anti-gazumping insurance for about £15 for £400 of cover which reimburses legal and surveying costs should you be gazumped.

EXCLUSIVITY OR 'LOCKOUT' AGREEMENT

To further safeguard against gazumping, a buyer can ask the vendor to sign a pre-contract exclusivity or 'lockout' agreement, which can be arranged by a solicitor and typically costs approximately £100. This legally binding agreement between the buyer and seller states that during a specified period, usually around a fortnight, the vendor will take the property off the market and not enter into any agreement with another party otherwise the buyer is entitled to compensation. In return the buyer is expected to stick to a strict timetable. There is no obligation to exchange contracts at the end of the lockout.

Such agreements have become increasingly popular, especially since the Court of Appeal ruled in 1993 that a vendor breaking one is liable for breach of contract.

Such agreements only protect the buyer and therefore estate agents and solicitors would usually not recommend a vendor enter into one. Even so, as lockout agreements are in force for only two weeks or so, they can be popular with sellers as they encourage a swift sale. If the sale then collapses, little time has been lost.

IF COMPLETION DOES NOT TAKE PLACE

If the seller decides not to complete, the buyer has the legal right to cancel the contract, recover his deposit and interest and take legal proceedings against the seller for the loss. This could include costs relating to such things as the extra expense incurred for finding a similar property, legal costs, renting a temporary home and compensation for the inconvenience.

If the buyer decides not to complete, the seller can cancel the contract in the same way and keep the deposit.

COMPLETION

As long as all goes smoothly, usually several weeks after exchange of contracts comes 'completion', when at last you can move into your new home.

BUYING IN NORTHERN IRELAND

Buying property in Northern Ireland is generally similar to buying in England and Wales but there are differences. The vendor's solicitor, rather than the buyer's, usually instigates the local authority 'searches' in order to establish that there are no planned developments or other such issues that could affect the property. The vendor pays for the searches.

Also, the contracts are not 'exchanged' but instead the vendor's solicitor provides the contract, which is then forwarded to the buyer's solicitor to be signed by the buyer. It is then returned to the vendor's solicitor and the vendor signs the contract to seal the deal.

BUYING IN SCOTLAND

Many properties in Scotland are sold through solicitors' property centres rather than through estate agents. It is common to arrange a viewing of the property through the seller's solicitor.

Rather than make offers below the asking price, as is common in England and Wales, buyers usually make offers *over* a certain price as properties in Scotland are mainly advertised on this basis. This has increasingly meant that in particularly popular areas a property can sell for significantly more than the asking price. Offers are made in the form of a sealed bid and as you don't know how much other prospective buyers are offering, you have to be prepared that there's every chance you won't be successful. You cannot attempt to secure the property by making a bid of '£100 more than the highest offer you receive'. Sometimes, property is sold at a fixed price, and the first person to offer it secures the property.

Most Scottish property, whether a flat or house, is not owned freehold or leasehold but on 'feudal tenure', which means that they are owned in the same way as a freehold home except that the original owner (the 'superior') may have imposed conditions or restrictions on the use of the land or buildings, which are in force in perpetuity. These could include a ban on commercial use or upon building an extension, for example. The property offered for sale is sometimes referred to as 'the feu'.

You need a Scottish solicitor to buy in Scotland and the Law Society of Scotland can provide details of ones in your area. It is not a good idea to contemplate doing the conveyancing yourself in most circumstances. When you have found a property and are ready to make an offer, inform your solicitor who will tell the seller's solicitor of your intention to buy.

In Scotland once you have made an offer for a property you cannot pull out, as you are permitted to do elsewhere in the UK. Therefore, you need to have your finance and survey sorted out before you make an offer. This means that if the vendor does not accept your offer your surveying and other fees are lost.

English buyers who have experienced gazumping would undoubtedly be fans of the more rigid Scottish system, although it causes significantly more buyers to have to arrange bridging loans and to move to temporary accommodation.

Offers in Scotland are increasingly being submitted with longer and longer lists of extra conditions and therefore this usually entails a bigger delay before the offer is accepted, which increases the chance of gazumping taking place.

If, having made your offer and it is accepted, problems arise such as difficulties unearthed in the land search, the vendor would have to rectify the problem or otherwise would be liable for damages.

Once the deal is agreed, completion is usually far speedier than elsewhere in Britain. The written offer and subsequent correspondence relating to it are known as 'the missives', which is the Scottish equivalent of exchanging contracts. No deposit is required but missives are legally binding, and both buyer and seller are liable to damages should they withdraw.

Because you are legally committed to the purchase when making the offer, if you are selling in England, Wales or Northern Ireland in order to buy in Scotland you must be careful not to find yourself in the position where you have accepted an offer to buy your property that is not legally enforceable, but are legally bound to buy the property you have put an offer on in Scotland.

In some areas of the Scottish market, chiefly in crofting areas, largely in the Highlands and Islands, buyers have been discouraged by land reform plans by the Scottish parliament. The 2003 Land Reform (Scotland) Act has given crofters and tenanted farmers the right to buy 2.5 million acres of land as well as giving the public access to 15 million acres of land.

In affected areas, it is important to take advice from a local chartered surveyor who can fully research the situation concerning the rights of crofters and tenants before buying. Yet many so-called crofter's cottages have already been de-crofted and their land would not be affected by such legislation.

For more information on the Scottish system contact the Law Society of Scotland. The Council of Mortgage Lenders has a booklet on buying in Scotland, also available on its website.

BUYING AT AUCTION

An alternative route to finding your dream home is to buy through a property auction. Once chiefly the domain of developers and commercial buyers, auctions selling residential properties of all types have become increasingly popular in recent years.

At auctions you can often find unusual properties that seldom crop up at conventional high street estate agents, such as pubs that could be converted to residential use being disposed of cheaply in batches by breweries, and ex-branches of banks being closed as telephone and Internet banking gain in popularity.

Auctions are traditionally seen as a good source of property bargains, for a number of reasons. A property may be difficult to sell because of blight (such as subsidence or being on an ugly, busy road) or fire damage, or by having a sitting tenant. It may be sold on the instructions of the executors or beneficiaries of a will. A quick sale may be required, the property may be unusual and therefore difficult to value, it may be a repossession, it may be owned by an organisation, housing association or local authority and be surplus to requirements or simply in need of modernisation or repair.

Property auctions have long been seen as an oasis of bargains, but they have become so popular in recent years that an increasing number of properties are greatly exceeding their reserve prices. Indeed, at the time of writing, a tiny derelict building in Shropshire with no land or opportunity to convert with an auction guide price of £5,000 sold for £27,200. This is by no means exceptional. The possibility of getting carried away and bidding well over the current market value is more of a possibility than ever.

Guide prices are often purposefully lowered by auctioneers to generate extra interest and lure buyers, although valuing property is not an exact science and properties valued by estate agents also often sell at substantially above the asking price, especially in times of a buoyant economy.

Before bidding for a property you should ask the auctioneer how he defines his guide price. With some auctioneers the guide price is what he thinks the property will sell for. It may be a figure linked to what the reserve is. A guide price that looks low often indicates that the reserve price is low too.

One cause of the value of lots greatly exceeding expectations is the sheer lack of good property and a bigger and bigger pool of eager buyers. Many buyers have emerged now auctions have lost their stigma for being dominated by professional property investors taking advantage of the many repossessed properties emerging in auction rooms in the early 1990s.

An increasing number of people are attending auctions to avoid the spectre of gazumping, where you lose the property you have agreed to buy because another buyer offers a higher price. At auction, you know that when the hammer falls you have an unalterable price to pay. You cannot be gazumped.

Some auction properties attract fifty or more prospective buyers. To succeed at buying at auction you have to be organised and not half-hearted, getting your survey and the finance arranged in advance.

Once the hammer has fallen on your bid you have to pay an immediate deposit, typically 10 per cent of the value of the property, with 28 days to complete. This can be a problem in itself, as many lenders are taking longer than this to process applications.

It's a quick, efficient and, most of the time, cost effective way of buying because you're cutting out middlemen and speeding up the legal process. You exchange at the auction instead of waiting months and months in chains.

Auctions have also greatly grown in popularity because of the unbeatable speed of the transaction. Buyers and sellers, disillusioned with solicitors who may move at a snail's pace, the indecision from those they buy and sell from and the stresses of a property chain, are flocking to the auction rooms instead.

Even if a property bought at auction goes for the guide price and appears beyond doubt to be a bargain, it still might not be. People often assume that auctioned properties are usually in a bad state of repair, and although this is often not the case, the catalogue description is brief and may not mention that the property has subsidence, a sitting tenant, a short lease or that the garden backs on to a motorway.

With possibly many other people viewing the property you're interested in and maybe just two weeks from publication of the catalogue and auction day, the motivation to have a survey done is often far lower than it should be. Many buyers take a chance on auctioned property, and the result can be being landed with a property that needs extensive renovation and ends up being a major financial drain rather than the bargain it first seemed. Also, banks and building societies could decline mortgage applications if the home is in a bad condition, leaving you with a huge debt if you have had your bid accepted.

Prospective purchasers should visit a couple of auctions to understand the auction process before considering buying this way.

If you see a property in a catalogue that you like, at the very least take a builder along when you view initially. Check on auction day that the property has not been withdrawn or sold in advance. Arrive early at the auction to get a good seat – and be prepared to lose.

You should write down the maximum figure you can stretch to, and when they get to that figure in the auction, leave the room. If you are successful, arrange buildings insurance from the date of the auction.

The Essential Information Group collates data provided by 104 auction houses across the UK and provides auction-related services including AuctionWatch, which searches catalogues nationwide for the type of property you are looking for, for around £70 per quarter.

HOUSE SWAPPING

Swapping rather than selling your home can mean having to pay just £5 in stamp duty. The downside to swapping rather than selling your house is the extra difficulty in finding someone happy to make a swap, and also in reaching agreement of the extra amount needed to be paid by one party if one property is worth more than the other, as is likely.

For example, if a house worth £350,000 is being swapped for a house worth £250,000 plus the cash difference of £100,000, special rules apply to the cheaper of the two properties being swapped as the tax authorities see the transaction as a transfer and the cheaper house is therefore only liable for a £5 fixed duty. The duty is still payable on the more expensive house, but savings can be split between the swappers.

In the above example, buying traditionally rather than swapping, stamp duty at 3 per cent or £7,500 is payable on the £250,000 property and therefore £7,495 is saved.

One website, **www.webswappers.com**, has successfully paired up individuals willing to swap their homes, and saved them thousands of pounds in stamp duty in the process. Swappers can place their property swap on the site for free, or for £65 a 'for swap' sign can be put outside the property and a digital photograph of the property taken.

USEFUL TELEPHONE NUMBERS/EMAIL ADDRESSES

PROFESSIONAL PROPERTY FINDERS

The County Homesearch Company: 01872 223349; Homecare Consultants: 01494 447295; Compass Relocation: 01233 813535; Stacks Relocation: 01666 860523; Country Choice: 01672 562252; Finders Keepers: 01344 891971.

DIY CONVEYANCING

Oyez: 0870 737 7370

BUYING IN SCOTLAND

Estate agents with a good range of Scottish property include: Cluttons, 01292 268181; C.K.D. Finlayson Hughes, 01463 224343; MacArthur Stewart, 01546 602424; Bell Ingram, 01863 766683 and F.P.D. Savills, 01356 628600.

BUYING AT AUCTION

Essential Information Group: 020 7720 5000

Auctioneers include: Allsop and Co, 020 7494 3686; Clive Emson Auctioneers, 0891 517744; Edwin Evans, 020 7228 5864; Winkworth Auctions, 020 8649 7255; Countrywide Property Auctions, 0870 240 1140; Barnard Marcus, 020 8741 9990; Sullivan Mitchell, 01590 677555; F.P.D. Savills ,020 7824 9091; Strettons Chartered Surveyors, 020 8520 9911.

8 MOVING IN

PREPARING FOR MOVING DAY

MOVING COUNTDOWN

With a month to go . . .

- book the removal firm if applicable
- arrange time off work and someone to look after children/pets
- obtain packing boxes and start filling them – with clear labelling on the outside. Put books in small boxes as large ones will be difficult to lift
- start filling out the change of address boxes on any bills you pay
- chuck out unwanted clutter. Some removal firms operate the OXBOXX scheme, where your unwanted goods are delivered to Oxfam on moving day
- arrange your final telephone bill at your old home and a new connection at your new one

With a week to go ...

- arrange for professional disconnection of appliances you are removing like a gas cooker
- arrange for final reading of gas, water and electricity supplies and to take over utility accounts at the new property
- cancel direct debits/standing orders connected with your old home (such as gas, electricity and mortgage) and begin new ones at your new home
- cancel milk/newspaper deliveries and so on and pay the final bills
- remove fitted items like mirrors, pictures, shelves and so on

Assuming that the sale goes through to completion without difficulty, there is still plenty to do between exchange of contracts and moving in. To start with, it's a good opportunity to clear out rubbish from the loft or the garage and sell anything of any value at a car boot sale or donate to charity.

You can start obtaining quotes from removal companies. Being flexible about dates can help get the price down. Mondays, Tuesdays and Wednesdays are usually cheaper. Will you do the packing yourself or leave it to them? If you do it yourself, label the boxes clearly with the contents and the room they will be going into.

CHANGE OF ADDRESS

Wait until contracts have been exchanged before you notify anyone of the change of address in case the sale falls through.

Website **www.ihavemoved.com** offers a free change-of-address service and lists all the companies you should notify of your move such as utilities, magazine subscriptions, the DVLA and the passport office. All you do is key in your old and new addresses, tick the organisations you wish to notify and the website does the rest. The sites also provide free instant quotes for things like cleaning, conveyancing, surveying and removal companies.

Inform the following of your change of address: gas, electricity, water and telephone companies; insurance companies (contents, buildings, car and life insurance); bank and building societies; doctor, dentist and optician; employer; pension provider; loan companies; credit and store card companies; the Driver and Vehicle Licensing Authority (DVLA); council tax departments at both homes; national savings and premium bonds; TV licensing department; electoral register; schools; the Inland Revenue; the Department of Social Security; organisations you have subscriptions with.

Contact Royal Mail (**www.royalmail.com**) to arrange for it to forward your post to a new address, for up to two years for personal mail.

FINDING A GOOD REMOVAL FIRM

Expect to pay around £400–£650 for a professional removal firm to move the average contents of a three-bedroom house to an address locally, based on you doing the packing, with another £100–£150 when the packing is done for you.

When the removal company comes to quote for the work be sure to show everything that is to be moved. It's easy to forget an attic or garden shed stuffed with boxes, and it can be an unwelcome shock if the extra cost for these only emerges on moving day. Homes that have been altered so that furniture that originally went in can't be removed easily plus cumbersome, heavy objects, like a piano on the first floor, will bump up the price.

Do you want them to take down curtains, dismantle self-assembly beds and furniture, and fixtures and fittings? These usually need to be quoted for and will cost extra. Do you have unstraightforward items like antiques, pets, plants or a wine collection?

Insurance for the move will generally cost about 10 per cent above the total moving cost but is recommended. Check the small print in the policy. Is 'new for old' cover offered or only indemnity cover? Items you pack yourself will generally not be covered.

Hiring a van with driver may be around £150 or you could simply hire a Luton or transit van for the day for around £60–£90.

If you are tempted to do it all yourself, it may be a false economy when you take into account time off work, the cost of materials, van hire and labour costs. There could also be risks of damage and unforeseen hitches.

Charges by professional removal firms can vary considerably so shop around for an experienced firm that can offer a competitive quote.

Use a removal firm accredited to the National Guild of Approved Removers and Storers or the British Association of Removers. The latter can provide free advice for planning your move and can recommend removal companies in your area. Most B.A.R. members offer insurance against breakages and other mishaps and Careline offers a 24-hour service that deals with problems that may arise up to the move and for three months after, such as a leaking roof.

Ask removal companies what insurance they have against damage. Is there a charge for loan of boxes and other packaging? How much work are you required to do in preparation? Bear in mind that many removal firms will not accept a booking until contracts have been exchanged in case the sale falls through.

Will the van be able to access your street? Ensure there is adequate parking and inform the removal firm of any parking restrictions, poor access, spiral staircases and other potential difficulties in advance.

Removers are not permitted to interfere with mains services, so contact gas, electricity and water companies well in advance of the move.

You will need to have someone available to oversee what is being moved at both addresses. A clear plan showing where you want furniture placed allows the removers to put it exactly where you want it rather than leaving you with another job to do.

The Internet can help. **www.helpiammoving.com** gives guidance on moving home and to-do lists and a search facility for removal companies. **www.reallymoving.com** can provide online quotes from removal firms and other services, including an unpacking service where from under £200 for a one-bedroom flat a team will unpack and set up everything, even connecting computers and TVs, build shelves and assemble flat packs.

The Box Store (**www.theboxstore.co.uk**) sells self-assembly packing boxes, tape and bubble wrap kits from around £40. Order by 4 p.m. and a pack of boxes can be delivered the next day by A1 House Moving Box Ltd (**www.a1box.co.uk**).

JUST BEFORE THE MOVE

AT YOUR OLD HOME Disconnect the cooker and washing machine and defrost the freezer. Check that your solicitor has arranged for the new owner to take over the council tax bill. Notify your electricity, gas, water and telephone companies of the move. Cancel the paper and milk deliveries.

AT YOUR NEW HOME Are there any guarantees or service agreements relating to the property that you will be taking over? Will you be receiving keys for all of the locks in the property, from front door to garden shed?

MOVING DAY

Take electricity and gas meter readings and read the water meter if there is one at your old address. Ask for a final telephone bill. Arrange connection of gas and electricity at your new address and read the meters. Leave a set of keys with your estate agent at your old property and label the spares. Make sure important documents and emergency numbers are accessible. Leave pre-addressed labels so that new owners can send on any mail that hasn't been redirected. Lock all windows and doors before leaving.

A kettle, washing-up gloves, washing-up liquid, teabags, milk, a couple of mugs and some biscuits should be easily accessible for when you arrive at your new home ... as well as a bottle of champagne if it all goes smoothly, and a packet of Prozac and a bottle of gin if it doesn't!

It is an unwritten rule not to remove things like light bulbs and light fittings, door handles, fireplaces, fitted cupboards or anything cemented down or planted in the garden.

You should leave the property in the condition in which the buyer first saw it, but cleared of all the items that were not included in the purchase price or bought separately by the purchaser.

Be careful not to leave anything as the new owner would be able to claim they are now his, making it very difficult to recover them.

WILLS

You should either make a will or update your existing one as soon as you become a property owner.

SECURING YOUR HOME

CRIME PREVENTION MEASURES

Crime prevention has advanced greatly in recent years, with increasingly sophisticated alarms coming as standard. But there are a number of other, comparatively inexpensive measures you can take to protect your belongings. Microdots the size of a pinhead and printed with a unique personal identification number can be painted with a small brush. Alphascientific and Identidot (www.identidot.com) have a microdot homepack at £24.95 including post and packing.

A company called SmartWater manufactures kits from £350 containing a harmless solution that leaves a chemically coded 'fingerprint' on objects that is only visible under ultraviolet light. It may sound expensive, but can treat around 350 items.

If you have valuable furniture or antiques, microchips can be injected into upholstery or into a tiny hole drilled into the back of a picture frame. Microchips are available mail order at £5 each inclusive from AVID. The Thesaurus Active Crime Tracking System is the world's largest searchable database of stolen art and antiques.

Security marker pens, whose invisible ink is legible only under ultraviolet light, are widely available at DIY shops. Such measures are very worthwhile, as the police routinely examine recovered property for marking.

If you're going away, cancel the regular deliveries – but be careful not to advertise the fact to the whole shop when you're doing so. And if you take a taxi to the airport, you have no idea how law abiding the taxi driver is. Consider walking around the corner, arranging to be picked up away from the house.

The new generation of alarm systems with do-it-yourself installation are wire-free and therefore easier to install than ever. DIY alarms are widely available from DIY shops, starting from under £100.

Monitored systems, where alarms are continuously monitored by a central headquarters and emergency services summoned in the case of emergency, represent one of the fastest growing sectors of the home security market. ADT, for example, typically charges around £500 for installation of its systems and around £25 monthly for monitoring.

Simple measures like arranging for a neighbour to regularly visit and monitor your property, and maybe park on your drive, when you go on holiday can make all the difference. Participating in neighbourhood watch schemes can dramatically reduce crime in a neighbourhood.

Although you can never make your home completely secure, you can make it so much trouble that the casual thief will move on to the next property. Prickly bushes, noisy gravel and large, cumbersome window boxes with large plants can all help deter a burglar. Ladders, tools and climbing frames left around the garden can help a thief.

You can arrange for your local crime prevention officer to visit for free and advise on security measures specific to your home. Two booklets, *How to Secure Your Home* and *A Secure Garden*, are produced by the Metropolitan Police, and most other police authorities provide leaflets on the subject. For tips on home security visit **www.met.police.uk/crimeprevention**.

HOUSE-SITTERS

Growing crime fears have also seen the growth of house-sitting agencies, which arrange for thoroughly vetted sitters to live in your home while you're away. Typically costing from about £25 per day, they are especially popular with pet owners, who prefer their animals to be cared for at home while they are on holiday.

The house-sitter simply visits beforehand to see how everything works and the animals' requirements and then moves in while you're away. If you have three small animals it usually works out at a similar cost to putting them in kennels, and so you have someone in your home at no extra cost.

FIRE PREVENTION AND PROTECTION

Your local fire service can provide advice about this. At the very least fit a smoke alarm conforming to the British Standard on each floor. The cheapest, ionisation alarms are sensitive to smoke from flaming fires, while optical alarms are better at detecting smouldering fires. The Association of Building Engineers produces a leaflet on fire protection.

INSURING YOUR HOME

In the excitement of buying a home, the rather uninspiring subject of insurance is unsurprisingly often not put on top of the 'to do' list. Although insurance may be about as interesting as watching the paint dry on the newly decorated walls of your new abode, it becomes vital when catastrophe strikes, such as the roof caving in.

Insurance policies vary greatly, even when you're getting identical cover, so be sure to get several quotes for each type of

insurance. A good way of searching for insurance is by surfing the net using websites like **www.rapidinsure.co.uk,
www.axa-direct.co.uk, www.churchill.co.uk, www.cis.co.uk,
www.cornhill.co.uk, www.directline.co.uk,
www.eaglestardirect.co.uk, www.endsleigh.co.uk, www.find.co.uk,
www.simplydirect.co.uk** and **www.swinton.co.uk**.

Be sure to check the small print of any policies you consider. Definitions and cover can vary greatly.

There are two main types of household insurance, buildings and contents. Buildings insurance covers the building itself, its fixtures and fittings, garden walls and fences. Contents insurance covers everything else, things that you would take with you if you moved.

Your mortgage deal may include a condition that you buy the lender's insurance, otherwise buy directly from an insurance company, an insurance Internet site (which is usually slightly cheaper) or an insurance broker. An insurance tax of 5 per cent is added to all premiums.

Brokers can be especially helpful if you are not a straightforward insurance risk, for example if you live in a high crime area or the property is liable to flooding or subsidence. Brokers can also help if you need to make a claim. A few offer an Internet presence. For more information on insurance brokers contact the British Insurance and Investment Brokers Association.

By increasing the excess (the amount you pay on any claim) slightly, the cost of insurance policies can reduce surprisingly, so ask how much the premium would be if you took the highest excess and compare.

BUILDINGS INSURANCE

Not only is it extremely unwise to omit to take out buildings insurance – which pays for repairing or rebuilding your home should it be destroyed in a fire or other calamity – but you will be required to have this insurance if you have a mortgage. Your mortgage lender may offer to provide this insurance, and sometimes, though less and less frequently, it may insist you take out its cover.

The cost of the premium relates to the cost of rebuilding your home from scratch. Buildings insurance is for the rebuilding cost rather than for the value of the property, which may be very different.

This can be difficult to work out but your lender will state how much to insure for, otherwise there may be a figure in your survey if you had one done, your insurance company may be able to help,

or log on to the Association of British Insurers website,
www.abi.org.uk, which has a table that can be used. The insurance
should commence before you take ownership of the property.

If you live in a flat, there will be a communal insurance policy
covering the whole building, for which you pay a share.

Policies generally cover eventualities like flood, fire and water
damage and may include malicious acts, like vandalism. You can
add on extras like accidental damage, and legal protection covering
legal fees in the event of a legal dispute. For the policy to remain
valid, it is important to fulfil all the requirements of the policy,
which may be very specific, for example fitting a certain standard of
lock. Check the strength of the door or window locks are fitted to –
a good lock on rotten wood is useless.

Areas prone to flooding or subsidence may incur higher
insurance costs. Combining buildings and contents insurance may
attract a discount as may joining a neighbourhood watch scheme
or installing a burglar alarm system. The insurer may require that
the alarm is installed by a company registered with the National
Approval Council for Security Systems (N.A.C.O.S.S.).

CONTENTS INSURANCE

Contents insurance can be of two types. The cheaper is indemnity,
where your contents are insured for their current worth. Therefore
a camera would be valued as being second-hand. Pricier is new-
for-old cover, where your contents are insured for what it would
cost to replace them.

You can pay extra for accidental cover, which covers anything you
break yourself, and you can also pay extra for all-risks cover to
insure possessions outside the home.

Make a detailed inventory of everything you own and try to work
out the value as accurately as possible because if you under-insure
your claims will not be met in full and if you over-insure, you are
wasting money. Take pictures around the home: if you have a
collection of 1,000 CDs, a photograph of them in your home goes
some way to convincing your insurer of such a collection in the
event of a claim.

If you have some particularly valuable items such as antiques or
collectables which could be difficult to value, consider using a
professional valuer (advertised in the Yellow Pages) or contact an
auction house. Specialist antique dealers may be able to help.
Contact trade associations such as the British Antique Dealers
Association, Lapada and the Society of Fine Art Auctioneers.

There are lots of add-ons you can buy covering such things as
family legal expenses, garden furniture, freezer contents, plants,

cash and replacement of lost or stolen keys and having locks changed.

If you are not taking contents insurance out for the first time, remember to have your existing cover transferred to your new address. The terms of the policy may change, or your new property may not meet the requirements of the policy. For instance, the locks may not be of a high enough standard. Front, side and back door locks should be changed as a matter of course.

INSURING THE MOVE

The removal firm, if you are using one, should have insurance for your possessions, but it is a good idea to also contact your insurance company to try and get temporary cover through your contents insurance policy.

MOTOR INSURANCE

Don't forget this: your new address may be considered a higher or lower risk.

USEFUL TELEPHONE NUMBERS/EMAIL ADDRESSES

CHANGE OF ADDRESS

Royal Mail: 08457 740 740.

FINDING A GOOD REMOVAL FIRM

The Box Store: 0800 013 2161

CRIME PREVENTION MEASURES

ADT, 0800 010 999; Alphascientific, 0845 757 3329; AVID, 01825 791069; Indentidot, 0121 250 2250; SmartWater, 01952 222706; Thesaurus Active Crime Tracking System, 01983 826000.

HOUSE-SITTERS

Animal Aunts, 01730 821529; Housewatch, 01279 777412;
Homesitters, 01296 630730; Minders Keepers, 01763 262102
and The Sitting Service, 01422 368692.

CONTENTS INSURANCE

Professional valuers include:
Gurr Johns, 020 7670 1111; Weller King, 01903 816633;
Wellington Personal Insurances, 020 7929 2811; David Ford,
01483 810230.

9 LOOKING AFTER YOUR HOME

MAINTAINING YOUR HOME

CUTTING COSTS

There are many ways to cut costs once you've moved in and it is surprising how many people are content to pay over the odds year after year when a quick telephone call and filling out a form can net considerable savings.

Major savings can be made by closely monitoring your mortgage. Even with remortgaging costs taken into account, it can pay huge dividends to investigate alternative mortgage packages on a regular basis.

Use insurance renewal dates as an opportunity to fish for cheaper quotes. But make sure you are comparing like with like policy-wise.

Consider switching gas and electricity suppliers. Energy watchdog OFGEM has a leaflet comparing tariffs. Consider changing your telephone company too.

Check your council tax. If you live alone, you are entitled to a 25 per cent reduction and as children under eighteen or those still in full-time education are not counted, a single parent may qualify. Also, if you suspect that your property is in too high a banding for the tax, contact your local council to try and get it reduced.

Choose energy-efficient appliances like washing machines and refrigerators, rated from 'A' for very energy efficient to 'G', which is least efficient. The annual savings can be surprisingly big for the more efficient models.

FURNISHING YOUR HOME

Raising the deposit, finding a mortgage and managing to land an affordable property are formidable hurdles in themselves, but once you've moved into your first home the costly task of furnishing it from scratch then usually presents itself.

It is important to research furniture shops and the deals they offer carefully as these can vary considerably. Store cards should often be avoided, as borrowing interest rates can be high. Taking out a loan with the shop in question is likely to be cheaper but it can often be worth taking out a personal loan with your bank for a lump sum to finance everything. And being able to pay cash can be more of a bargaining tool if you are able to haggle.

Look out for credit cards with interest-free introductory offers. Put the purchase on the plastic for the length of the interest-free period, and as long as you can pay off the balance when it ends, it's an excellent hassle-free deal that's hard to beat.

Another option, as long as your lender will agree, is borrowing an amount on top of the purchase price of the property. You will certainly have low monthly payments compared to a personal loan but you will be paying for your furniture and interest on the loan for the life of the mortgage, typically 25 years, so it won't be paid off until long after your settee has gone to that sofa workshop in the sky. Also, the greater the deposit you can pay and less you need to borrow, the better the mortgage deals tend to be.

It's a good idea to check out each retailer's website before visiting their shop. The larger companies all now have comprehensive websites with plenty of pictures and details of their ranges, often with measurements. Some even tell you whether the item you want is in stock, which can save a wasted journey.

Also, check whether the store you're buying from offers free delivery. That sofa may not seem such a bargain if you have to pay an extra £40 to have it delivered. Be prepared for a surprisingly long wait for larger items of furniture. It is not uncommon to have to wait eight, ten or even twelve weeks for sofas, for example.

Pretty high up on most new homeowners' shopping lists after the property itself must come the sofa. *The Weakest Link*'s Anne Robinson recently said that sofas are harder to choose than husbands. And there certainly is something in that, because there are such an overwhelming lot of types out there.

It is well worth choosing a sofa that has removable, easily washable covers as furniture gets grubby surprisingly quickly and without such covers it just takes some drunken mate to spill red wine one evening to lumber you with an expensive cleaning bill, possibly from a specialist steam clean company. It's an extra boon if you choose a fabric that can be thrown in the washing machine rather than requiring an expensive visit to the dry cleaners.

A spare bedroom is a luxury few can afford and so it makes a lot of sense to invest in a sofa bed so you have the option of being able to put friends and family up occasionally. Sofa bed designs vary enormously and some are amazingly cumbersome to transform into a bed, so be sure to try ones that interest you right there in the shop.

Futons work especially well in more modern homes, and as they fold out simply rather than outwards into a six-foot bed like a conventional sofa bed, they are ideal where space is scarce.

FURNITURE RETAILERS:

Habitat (0845 60 10 740, **www.habitat.net**); The Futon Company (0845 609 4455, **www.futoncompany.co.uk**); Ikea (020 8208 5601, **www.ikea.co.uk**); Muji (020 7323 2208, **www.muji.co.jp**); Next (0845 600 7000, **www.next.co.uk**); MFI (0870 607 5093, **www.mfi.co.uk**); Argos (0870 600 3030, **www.argos.co.uk**); John Lewis (08456 049 049, **www.johnlewis.com**).

HOME MAINTENANCE

www.improveline.com and **www.homepro.com** both feature help on home improvements while **www.scoot.co.uk** and **www.yell.co.uk** (the website of the Yellow Pages) contain directories of trades and services.

FINDING A BUILDER

Even though they can set up in business and alter buildings in ways that could threaten many lives, anyone can say they are a builder. They're not monitored and don't need any qualifications to start trading. They can stick a postcard in a shop window and be bashing down a supporting wall the next day.

Therefore, to lessen the chances of stress and costly mistakes, it is important to choose your builder carefully. If you cannot get a recommendation from friends or family, opt for a firm belonging to a recognised trade association such as the Federation of Master Builders (F.M.B.). Don't just rely on a logo. Telephone the relevant association to be sure the firm is a member.

Choose a builder registered with a warranty scheme. The F.M.B. has a National Register of Warranted Builders and other insurance-backed guarantees are available.

www.findabuilder.com has a database of registered builders, and London Women and Manual Trades publishes a £5 directory listing London-based female tradespeople. **www.flyingtoolbox.com** lists over three hundred companies rated by customer opinion. The Royal Institute of British Architects offers a free client advisory service and can suggest suitable architects.

If structural work is involved, it is advisable to consult a structural engineer, surveyor or architect before undertaking the work.

Get a quotation in writing with a firm price for the job that cannot be varied. An estimate is only a rough guide. Write on it that you accept the quotation on the basis that it is a firm and definite price for the job.

Agree in writing a completion date for the work. If the work is not finished by this time you can claim compensation. If a completion date has not been agreed in advance and there are unreasonable delays you can stipulate when the work must be finished. If the work is not finished by then you can claim compensation for the cost of having the work done by another firm.

Even better, draw up a contract specifying the cost, completion date, length of working day and other details. The Stationery Office has a comprehensive ready-made contract with spaces to fill in the details of your project. If your builder refuses to sign a contract, it's pretty likely he's a cowboy.

The builder must carry out the work with reasonable care and skill, according to the Supply of Goods and Services Act. Materials used must be of acceptable quality. The builder is still responsible for the materials if the fault is due to a manufacturing defect and not his workmanship.

If the work is unacceptable, unless it is so bad you cannot entrust the builder to put it right, you should give the builder an opportunity to rectify things, otherwise any compensation you later claim may be reduced. If the builder is unable or unwilling to make the work acceptable he is in breach of contract but you will have to provide evidence showing that the work is not of a reasonable standard. You can do this by asking other contractors to state why it is unacceptable, and in the case of more major work a surveyor's report is recommended. Do not ask another builder to rectify the work until you have written proof of the shortcomings. You can claim compensation from your original builder for the cost of further work to put things right.

A scheme was launched in 2002 to protect consumers from cowboy builders. The Quality Mark scheme ensures that builders reach standards set by the government before they are allowed to be part of a register which can then be accessed by the public.

The scheme is free to use and ensures, among other things, that registered contractors are independently and regularly inspected by certification bodies and licensed by the Department of Trade and Industry. Any building work carried out is also automatically guaranteed for up to six years against loss of deposit, poor workmanship or major defects.

Standard easy-to-understand contracts are used and consumers have access to a complaint resolution system. The Quality Mark website is at **www.qualitymark.org.uk**.

Also, a database of traders is in development from the National Consumer Council and the Trading Standards Institute. It would carry lists of traders from mechanics to builders, and will be able to provide information about whether they were reputable.

WATER AND DRAINAGE

The Institute of Plumbing's website (**www.plumbers.org.uk**) provides a list of members by postcode, all conforming to its rigorous code of practice, and contains advice on dealing with various plumbing problems. **www.plumbers.uk.com** is like an Internet Yellow Pages, but its plumbers have not been vetted. For a plumber to appear on the website **www.whotouse.co.uk**, three customers have to write in with recommendations.

GAS

A service engineer has to be called to connect any new appliances to the gas supply.

The website for British Gas (**www.gas.co.uk**) contains some general advice.

If you smell gas, call Transco's free 24-hour helpline to report a leak, and they can also provide a list of local emergency contractors.

For central heating and boiler problems call the Council for Registered Gas Installers (CORGI), which has a database of CORGI-registered plumbers, or you could opt for the Institute of Plumbing, which also has a database of approved plumbers (see above).

If you hit problems contact the Gas Consumers' Council.

ELECTRICITY

For power cuts call 24Seven's free helpline, the number on your electricity bill or consult the phone book.

Only use contractors registered with professional associations, such as an electrician approved by the National Inspection Council for Electrical Installation Contracting (N.I.C.E.I.C.), the Electrical Contractors' Association or the Electrical Contractors' Association of Scotland. The guy down the pub may be cheaper, but you don't want the lights going on every time you use the hot water tap.

PESTS

For problems like a rat infestation, squirrels or pigeons in the attic, foxes or cockroaches, call your local council's pest control department or try the British Pest Control Association, which can provide a list of approved pest control companies.

Bats are a protected species and destroying a bat roost can make you liable for prosecution under the Wildlife and Conservation Act. More information about bats is available on the website **www.bats.org.uk**.

If you have a barn or outbuildings, bear in mind that many other types of wildlife are protected, including field mice, badgers, bees and the common toad. The Joint Nature Conservation Committee (**www.jncc.gov.uk**) has further details.

LEGAL PROBLEMS

DAMAGE TO YOUR PROPERTY

Anyone who enters your home and carelessly causes damage to your property or furniture and fittings is liable to pay compensation for any losses. You can bring a small claim in the county court to recover damages, and if you lose you do not have to pay the other side's costs. Yet proving your case can be difficult. You have to establish that damage has been done and who it was that did the damage, and your story is likely to differ from that of the person you are claiming against.

ACCESS AND EASEMENTS, BOUNDARIES AND LAND OWNERSHIP

Disputes over access, easements (short cuts across your property to a neighbour's property or land, or access to their drainage systems, water supplies and such on your land), boundaries and land ownership can be notoriously difficult to sort out. In a country where a man's house is his castle, whole chains of house moves have been held up and homeowners bankrupted by court cases over land disputes involving just a few inches of turf.

Whether you're a buyer or seller, access rights to a property or across a property and boundaries need to be clearly defined in the form of clear formal documentation. Whether a fence has been carelessly installed, or a greedy neighbour has tried to nick a little more space or a local farmer has sold you a barn but wants access across your land to reach his fields, the problem may visit you at the time of buying or selling and if you're the homeowner it could be a cause of great irritation in between.

If the matter disputed is not serious, it would be well to question whether you care enough to pay the legal fees, generate animosity and take on the extra stress in attempting to resolve the problem.

If the matter cannot be ignored, in the first instance study the plans to your land. If the land is registered, contact the Land Registry. If it is unregistered consult your title deeds, held by your mortgage lender or solicitor.

These will not necessarily give you an accurate guide to where your boundaries lie. Your solicitor may be able to help in simple cases, but a chartered surveyor, preferably a land specialist, will be able to give the best advice. Contact the Royal Institute of Chartered Surveyors' information service.

If, on the other hand, you are the accused party, it is up to your neighbour to prove their case. Ask your neighbour to involve a surveyor before taking the matter further.

Bear in mind that in Britain, if the owner of a piece of land has not claimed it back for twelve years (ten in Scotland) it legally becomes the neighbours' through 'adverse possession', or squatters' rights in other words. Therefore, even if the boundary to the side of your house looks wrong and the plans to your property suggest a different boundary, it may have become legal.

Make every effort to avoid legal action. Politely write to the other party. Try to be rational and come to an amicable solution. Moving the fence a few inches will invariably be far cheaper than arguing in court, where often in this sort of dispute both sides may end up paying their own costs. Furthermore, even if you win, your neighbour may not necessarily comply with the ruling.

Try appointing a mediator. Mediation UK can put you in touch with a local trained mediator who, at no charge, will visit you and your neighbour separately and then arrange for you to meet to work out a solution.

If you appear to have a case and all else fails, you can obtain an injunction from the county court, where you can also claim compensation for any inconvenience experienced. But beware, it can be a long and costly process. And lounging in the sun on a Sunday afternoon when your neighbour's pottering about next door may never be the same again after the animosity that has been caused.

If you come to sell, you have a legal obligation to be truthful and in no way misleading if prospective buyers ask whether there are any disputes with neighbours.

It is important to establish where boundaries lie before buying a property. If there are queries, it is the seller's responsibility to sort these out and the buyer should not have to pay for this.

Boundary hedges tend to be a shared responsibility. Look for any supporting pillars or posts on your side of the wall or fence, which may indicate they're yours and your responsibility. 'T' marks on a boundary line on a site plan indicate the wall or fence belongs to the owner of the property inside which the 'T' mark appears. A line of trees or a hedge does not necessarily indicate the extent of the property.

According to the law, if your neighbour's hedge, tree or bush overhangs your property you can prune it back as far as the boundary, but no more. But if the tree is under a preservation order, or if you live in a conservation area (your council can advise) you could be fined for pruning the tree. You may erect a fence up to one metre high facing a road or up to two metres elsewhere on your property.

TRESPASS

If your neighbours treat your garden as an extension of their own, or you have unwanted visitors on your land, your legal position is clear if they are adults. They have committed trespass and you can obtain an injunction from your county court to keep them off your land. Breaking the injunction could result in a fine or prison sentence.

If children trespass, things are less clear. You're unlikely to get an injunction against a child and parents aren't liable for children's trespass, but you have a stronger case to take their parents to court if they damage anything.

OTHER NUISANCES

The 1956 Clean Air Act does not apply to domestic gardens and therefore an occasional bonfire or barbecue cannot be subject to prosecution. Yet regular ones could be classed as an actionable nuisance. Noise from a homeowner regularly holding parties is another actionable nuisance and if a visit by the police doesn't solve the problem you can apply to the local county court.

THE GARDEN

GARDEN IMPROVEMENTS

Although adding extra features to the garden like swimming pools, tennis courts, tree houses and ponds can seem irresistible on paper, in practice there can be unforeseen problems and, in the case of swimming pools, crippling running costs. Make the wrong 'improvement' and a garden feature may even reduce the value and saleability of your home.

Although housebuyers are wary of anything watery inside a house – such as rising damp, wet rot and dodgy plumbing – a well-maintained pond in the garden can be a positive selling point, making your home stand out from the rest.

FRONT GARDEN PARKING

In areas where parking spaces are scant, paving over the flower beds at the front of the house can certainly be a convenience and for that reason may increase the value of your property, but you could alienate future potential buyers who believe such actions spoil the look of the property.

It is important to convert the garden sympathetically to preserve the look of the property and the street in the best possible light. You are required to apply to your local council, which typically charges several hundred pounds to grant permission and lower the kerb.

PONDS

A pond can transform a dull backyard, and creates its own microclimate for moisture-loving mosses and plants, and can attract frogs, toads, dragonflies and butterflies. Today's plastic pond liners, available from garden centres, start at under £40, so you can install a pond easily and quickly. You could also get a landscape gardener to design the pond and organise the installation.

Small ponds can suffer from cloudy water, slime and algae because the water cannot aerate properly. A filtration system or algicide can help in this instance. Shallow ponds can freeze up in the cold months or evaporate in the hottest ones, killing pond plants and fish. Too much shade and falling leaves can turn the water into a sludge. A pond needs a sheltered, sunny spot away from overhanging trees. If young children use the garden, wire or wooden fencing should be put around the pond.

TENNIS COURTS

Installing a tennis court appeals to many sporting types with sizeable gardens. Being a very sociable game, entertaining friends takes on a new dimension and you keep fit in the process. Hard courts are far more popular than lawn courts as they are considerably easier to maintain.

Surprisingly, tennis courts require planning permission and although they are not buildings as such, permission may be refused by the local council. Even if it isn't, councils can be very strict about what can seem to be minor details, such as the colour of the fencing around the court. The cheapest courts, plain black macadam with all fencing, markings and other extras, cost from about £13,000 and typically take around three weeks to install. A clay court with a watering system costs over £40,000.

Tennis courts are generally a greater attraction to potential buyers than swimming pools because they are cheap and easy to maintain, are usable throughout the year and there are not the safety considerations associated with pools and young children.

TREE HOUSES

Another garden feature that can require planning permission is the humble tree house. Although you may be innocently erecting one simply for your children to enjoy, your local council may consider that it causes an undesirable loss of privacy for your neighbours, in the same way many councils disapprove of roof terraces that provide an unbroken view of next door. If you make your kids a tree house and the council's planning department then asks you to submit a planning application, you would have no choice but to dismantle it should they refuse permission.

SWIMMING POOLS

Many people consider that the most desirable feature you can add to a garden is a swimming pool, but again care must be taken before choosing. A well-designed pool, enclosed so that it can be used all year, can be a fabulous asset to a home. Being enclosed, heating costs are drastically reduced. Oxfordshire company Lanzare, for example, supplies telescopic sliding pool enclosures as well as pool domes that can be removed in two hours for the summer months.

Select an unheated, uncovered outdoor pool and not only will it be redundant for most of the year but, being unprotected from the elements, it will require more work to keep it and the water in good condition. Prospective future buyers of your home may view it as an impediment of the property and be put off by the added cost of having it removed and the garden relandscaped.

The least expensive option for a pool is one that is above-ground, starting at around £2,000 for a 24 ft x 12 ft model. If you want an in-ground pool, self-build kits, from £5,000 upwards, are the cheapest option and for the experienced DIY'er only. The majority of private pools are in-ground pools using a one-piece plastic liner. These cost from around £10,000, while a newer option is the fibreglass pool, which costs from about £12,000 for a 30 ft x 14 ft model. The longest lasting pools are made from a concrete shell with steel reinforcement, and cost from £15,000.

Outdoor pools or those housed in detached garden buildings are usually treated as permitted developments, although you need to apply for planning permission if your home is listed, overlooked by neighbours or in a conservation area.

Heating methods include the use of an oil boiler, gas boiler or electrical heater. A heat exchanger can sometimes be installed to operate from your existing domestic boiler with low capital costs. A heat pump is popular, run by electricity, extracting heat from the air and transferring this to the pool.

Contrary to popular belief, you don't need a large pool to exercise in. Install a counter current unit, and a small pool will do fine. These units creates a current that enables you to swim as fast as you wish while remaining in the same place, like a sort of aquatic treadmill. Ensure that the unit complies with the latest safety regulations. Jetstream supplies such units ranging from about £1,400 to over £4,000. They make a 12 ft x 8 ft pool viable for exercising in.

Obtain at least three quotes from installers experienced in building similar pools. Ask to see examples of previous pool installations they have built and check out references. Before accepting a quote you should be clear that important considerations such as ease of site access, disposal of spoil, availability and location of main services, the subsoil, water table and all other extras have been taken into account.

SPATA (**www.spata.co.uk**) has an online information service, providing answers to technical problems and information on sourcing equipment and services and free literature; Pool Industry Promotion has a 32-page free *Ideal Pool Guide*.

MAKING YOUR HOME MORE ENERGY EFFICIENT

TIPS FOR ENERGY EFFICiENCY

You don't have to buy a modern home to enjoy far slimmer fuel bills. It's possible to cut as much as 40 per cent off annual costs by making just a few changes around your existing home. It's well worth the energy, as there are many ways to reduce consumption.

Even not leaving the TV and video on standby can save around £15 a year.

Some effective changes, like loft insulation (at least 8 inches thick is ideal, but avoid insulating below the cold water tank to stop it freezing over) or draught proofing around doors and windows (especially old sash windows) are inexpensive if you do the work yourself, which is simple and the materials can be bought from a DIY shop.

Further insulation is possible by filling in gaps in the floorboards with sealant or wood moulding, insulating below the floorboards on all floors and sealing between the skirting board and floor.

Insulate walls either externally or more cheaply and effectively with cavity wall insulation if your home has cavity walls, which are typical if built after 1930. If you're planning to replace the windows, consider installing low-emissivity glass or double glazing. A DIY window seal film applied to existing windows is a cheap alternative. Buy fully lined curtains or sew lining fabric into existing ones.

A damp-proof membrane (about £15 for a 8 metre roll from DIY shops) fitted across the rafters in the loft prevents moisture getting in and radiates heat back into the house.

Unfortunately, many housebuilders believe that most buyers aren't prepared to pay extra for homes that exceed the bare minimum government levels in energy efficiency. It is a pity, as adding 5 per cent to construction costs can add a gigantic level of energy conservation, helping both the homeowner's pocket as well as world climate change and ecological damage.

Other energy-saving measures that can cut running costs surprisingly over time include choosing low energy light bulbs and energy-efficient domestic appliances.

Lag the hot water tank with an inexpensive 3 inch jacket and pipes wih foam pipe lagging from DIY stores. Turn your hot water thermostat down – it doesn't need to be scalding.

If you are on income support ask your local authority about possible grants. Free advice and possible grants towards energy saving can be obtained from your nearest Energy Advice Centre. The Council for Energy Efficiency Development can also provide advice.

CENTRAL HEATING

Long gone are the days when central heating was a rarity and the heights of sophistication were a 'coal-effect' three-bar electric fire in the centre of the living room, backed up by a rattling fan heater in the corner.

Installing central heating, at from around £2,500 for a three-bed semi, remains about the best way you can add value to your home. The current generation of central heating boilers, especially the energy-efficient condensing types, and to a lesser extent high-efficiency fan-assisted boilers, can considerably reduce fuel bills. Replacing a 15-year-old boiler can typically save 20 to 30 per cent on your fuel bills.

Fitting heating controls like a good boiler programmer, room thermostat or thermostatic radiator valves on individual radiators can slash bills even more. Thermostatic radiator valves allow you to control heating in individual rooms, which is especially good for rooms that tend to overheat like kitchens and conservatories or rooms that need extra heat briefly like bathrooms. Foil or a sheet of aluminium behind radiators will deflect warm air back into the room.

SOLAR POWER

In a bid to make as little impact as possible on world resources, there has been a huge increase in using eco-friendly ways to heat and light homes. Only a few years ago the idea of installing solar panels on your roof to harness the power of the sun was prohibitively expensive and seemed almost eccentric, yet today over 50,000 UK households now rely on solar systems to heat at least some of their hot water.

The majority of homes in Britain could use solar power, and systems start at around £2,500. Planning permission is seldom required unless you live in a conservation area or in a listed building. The water is warmed by the sun in a panel sited on a south-facing roof, or less commonly, in the garden. The water is then piped to the hot water cylinder, supplemented by conventionally heated water in the colder seasons.

If you are considering installing a solar energy system, ask a lot of questions about where it will be sited and how effective it will be. The systems being used vary enormously.

The British Photovoltaic Association can advise about solar heating.

FIREPLACES

If you plan to install a new fireplace it is important to bear in mind the proportions of the room so that the fire is in proportion and in keeping with the room. Establish the age of your property: a Georgian fireplace may look pretty in the antique shop, but not so attractive in an Edwardian home.

For traditionalists, the most expensive component of the fireplace is the surround, which could be marble, wood or stone. Costs can be cut by searching architectural salvage firms. If you are installing a gas flame-effect fire, a gas pipe is run to the fire basket and should be installed by a registered CORGI gas fitter.

If you use an open fire or heating appliance it is crucial to have the chimney swept regularly, which typically costs from about £40 to £90 per chimney. Not only does the fire burn more efficiently but a badly maintained chimney is a fire risk which could lead to structural damage and also could bring the threat of lethal carbon monoxide fumes. A fireguard with protective mesh is a legal requirement for open fires if children are present. Contact the National Association of Chimney Sweeps to find your nearest sweep.

For people living in smokeless zones (check with your local authority's environmental service department to see if there are restrictions) a solid fuel-burning stove is an excellent option. They are easy to install into an existing fireplace or where there is access to an external ventilation pipe, although planning permission is occasionally needed so check with your local building inspector. They can provide a huge boost of heat as the heat is retained in the stove rather than disappearing up the chimney. A couple of decades ago there was little choice and few installers, but today there are some stunning models that can transform a room beautifully. The cheapest, usually traditional, are cast iron, but there are also stainless steel modern ones and extra-efficient tiled ones from Scandinavia.

REDUCING ALLERGENS AND CHEMICAL IRRITANTS IN YOUR HOME

In Britain over three million people are currently affected by asthma, a fourfold increase in the last thirty years, and many more are affected by other allergic conditions. Fortunately, there are steps that those suffering from asthma and allergies can take in the home to help prevent triggering them.

Although buying a property that requires major renovation or structural repair can be tempting for the financial rewards refurbishment can bring, the work can cause a lot of dust and other irritant triggers, so for the asthma sufferer selecting a home that is in good condition is usually preferable. As far as possible, avoid old or damp accommodation, or that which is near rivers or canals.

As well as the dust and fumes of general building work, problems can arise when treating a house for things like woodworm and moulds. Wet paint gives off chemicals that trigger a lot of people with asthma and allergies. Use non-solvent-based paints such as water-based paints or opt for wood panelling. On the floor use tiles, sealed cork or wood or lino. Cavity wall insulation containing formalin and formaldehyde should be avoided as they can cause adverse effects. Micafil is free of these chemicals. Formaldehyde is also present in chipboard, kitchen units, carpets and open fires.

Houses with open gas fires and cookers have higher levels of nitrogen dioxide, which can exacerbate symptoms of asthma, than those without.

Vent tumble-dryers externally, dry washing outside if possible and avoid hanging washing on radiators, to reduce humidity.

House-dust mites are one of the most common triggers for those affected by asthma in Britain. The mites live in bedding, beds, soft toys and soft furnishings, so select leather, wood, plastic or cane furniture rather than upholstered furniture that can harbour dust more readily. Indeed, think minimalist throughout the home: plain wooden bed frames are better than upholstered beds and bed boards.

If replacing curtains with shutters and blinds seems too drastic, washing curtains every three months is a compromise.

The less clutter there is, the less chance dust has to harbour around the building. Use anti-dust-mite covers to cover mattresses, pillows and duvets and wash them regularly at 60°C or more to kill the mites. Freeze soft toys weekly then wash in hot water to kill mites.

But there's no point spending time and money on such measures if mites, for example, aren't a trigger if you have asthma. Attend an allergy clinic in the first instance to establish your particular allergy triggers before making costly changes.

Many families affected by asthma consider selling up their city home to buy a home in the country, but this is not necessarily the solution. An international study of asthma and allergies in childhood recently found that the incidence of asthma in twelve- to fourteen-year-olds was higher in rural than urban areas. One reason could be because wind direction causes levels of ozone (summer smog) to be higher in the countryside than towns as the urban pollutants causing ozone, which are mainly from road traffic, reach their peak in rural areas. A Scottish Highlands study found asthma levels significantly higher than the national average on the Isle of Skye, which has no heavy industry and very little traffic and ozone.

Other measures that contribute towards a low allergy home include buying a high-filtration vacuum cleaner and not re-using vacuum cleaner bags or letting them overflow. Dusting with a damp cloth keeps dust out of the air.

In the garden avoid highly scented flowers and wind-pollinated plants such as grasses.

EXTENDING YOUR HOME

EXTEND OR MOVE?

Moving home isn't always the answer if you want more space. You may have put a lot of work into your garden and love it, or get on very well with your neighbours. If you live in an area where property prices are high, it is usually substantially cheaper to extend your present home – usually via the loft, basement or an extension – rather than move to a new home with the equivalent extra space. In areas where property prices are low, the cost differences are nothing as acute.

Generally, a successful extension that will add rather than lower value to a property will not be overdeveloped, or have a disproportionately small amount of land to the size of the building. It is also better to successfully build the extension in a complementary style rather than attempt to match the existing structure and fail.

Extending your home could put your home in a higher council tax band and is likely to result in higher insurance, light and heating costs. Also, converting a loft into a room robs you of storage space.

Don't embark on home improvements like an extension at the expense of household repairs that, if neglected, could jeopardise the structural integrity of the property.

Make sure that you have, and keep in a safe place, any guarantees and letters or certificates of authority for any building work carried out. If you change your mind about extending and decide to move, inform your estate agent as the property may be worth more if outline planning permission for conversion of an empty space has been obtained.

PLANNING PERMISSION

If you intend to carry out work on your home, consult your local planning authority to see whether you need planning permission, which is dependent upon the size and type of property and work to be done.

A planning application may be necessary for extensions, alterations, roof gardens, conservatories, loft conversions, balconies, garages, fences, walls, alterations to a previous planning consent or change of use (such as dividing a house into flats or a pub into a home), alterations to road access, off-street parking and drives.

Trees that you may want to fell may be covered by preservation orders or may be in conservation areas. Buildings which are Grade II listed require listed building consent from the relevant local authority, while consent is granted by English Heritage in the case of Grade I and II* listed buildings.

Article 4 Directions apply to some conservation areas and restrict permitted development rights. Designed to protect the appearance of a group of buildings, you need local authority permission to make changes to the facade of a building, which includes painting it, installing a satellite dish, installing uPVC windows or replacing the front garden with parking space. Conservation areas without Article 4s are less strictly controlled.

Planning departments have differing policies, and the stricter ones have been known to prohibit anything from tree houses to Wendy houses. Conservation areas, areas of outstanding natural beauty and national parks have specific controls. You may be eligible for a house improvement grant, and if you are extending minimally planning permission may not be necessary.

The Department of the Environment publishes a free booklet, *Planning Permission: a Guide for Householders*, and this is available from council offices. Their website also contains relevant information. They also publish a free booklet, *Planning Appeals*, which explains what to do if permission has been refused. The Royal Town Planning Institute has leaflets, advice and consultants on hand.

The crucial thing when extending is to satisfy building and planning regulations to the letter to avoid future problems and to ensure you have a safe living space. Also the design must be sympathetic with the current building: an ugly extension may increase the likelihood of problems selling in the future.

If you need planning permission you can draw up the plans yourself or use a professional such as a surveyor, an architect, or a consultant chartered town planner.

BUILDING REGULATIONS

Most extensions, structural alterations to existing buildings and new buildings are governed by Building Regulations (or in Scotland, Building Standards (Scotland) Regulations), which are generally concerned with building materials used, standard of workmanship, health and safety and fire precautions. You do not need to apply for Building Regulation approval where no structural work is involved, such as replacing drains or repairing a building. Contact the building control officer at your local authority for further advice.

USING AN ARCHITECT

Omit the services of an architect when you plan big building works on your home, and you may be courting disaster.

All but the craziest of us get the experts in when a spot of root canal work needs doing or the car needs a new exhaust, so it is strange that when it comes to extending the home, many people leave the design to their builders or attempt the design themselves on the back of a napkin.

Without an architect, as well as the stress of navigating the mysterious worlds of planning permission, building regulations and builder's tenders, of groundworks and first and second fixes, if it all goes wrong the final bill could be even more catastrophic than wearing green when everyone knows that the current season's colour is black.

An architect's fee, typically around £2,000 to £4,000 for a £40,000 job, but which may be as much as 20 per cent of the total, may seem steep but can save thousands of pounds more in the many mistakes and weeks of worry that can be avoided.

A good architect will discuss your needs in detail, iron out your sketchy, muddled ideas, advise whether your aspirations match your budget and will add or subtract value to the property, and can create a design that will be in keeping with your house.

He can inject artistic flair into the project and steer you away from ill-conceived designs that would incur the wrath of your neighbours, steal most of the borough's quota of sunlight, as well as damage the saleability of your property.

He will be able to prevent planning and building regulations problems with the local council which otherwise could drag on for many months.

Architects can also advise of good builders, draw up a contract for the schedule of building works and take the role of professional inspector, visiting the construction site regularly and certifying that in his professional opinion the works are to the required standard.

Personal recommendation is the best way to find an architect, otherwise the Royal Institute of British Architects (R.I.B.A.) Client Advisory Service can put you in touch with local ones. Invite a handful to give you a free consultation so you can sound out their ideas, fees and ways of working. Check out their past work and ask previous clients whether they were happy and the job came in at the cost quoted and within the agreed time frame.

To check you're dealing with a bona fide professional architect who comes complete with indemnity insurance, rather than a self-titled architectural designer, check with the Architects Registration Board.

Before the initial design brief, spend time building up a detailed checklist of requirements and give a copy to the architect so that he totally understands your needs. Be clear about your budget and be willing to compromise to keep to it.

Before contemplating major change to a period property you can get free advice from bodies such as the Georgian Group, the Victorian Society, English Heritage and the Society for the Protection of Ancient Buildings. The Architecture Foundation is a good contact for contemporary design and publishes guides to many of the best current architects, *New Architects* and *New Architects 2*, both £25.

Beware of architects with grandiose designs. It's easy to be seduced by these, but will your architect's idea of a gargantuan glass pyramid and water feature above the new study allow for more basic aspects of the job like plumbing and electricity?

Accept that his estimate for the cost of the building works is only that, and that when the job goes out for tender, builders' quotes may be higher, although a serious underestimation of costs is unacceptable. Details on how to find a good builder appear earlier in this chapter.

Agree fees with the builder and a strict schedule of deadlines for the work in writing. The R.I.B.A. has a useful document, 'Conditions of Appointment for Small Works', which, accompanied by a covering letter from the architect, should cover the work unless you're commissioning something on the large side like, say, a second Pompidou Centre.

If things go wrong, and differences cannot be settled by amicable discussion, the R.I.B.A. can arrange for a mediator to examine the facts in an attempt to sort things out before you resort to going to court.

Further information about architects is available from the Architects and Surveyors Institute, the Royal Incorporation of Architects in Scotland, the Royal Society of Architects in Wales and the Royal Society of Ulster Architects.

CABINS AND LODGES

Provided you have the land to accommodate it, a timber cabin or lodge is an inexpensive way to buy living space. Starting at around £8,000, these can usually be erected in a couple of days.

Check what is included in the price. Installation, double glazing, decoration, sanitary ware and electrical wiring are often included, while there may be extra costs for features like timber foundations, Velux roof lights, lighting and heating.

CONSERVATORIES

A conservatory on the side or back of your home can be a great asset, adding an extra room that is light and airy or doubling the size of a living room or kitchen.

But be cautious about cheaper structures. The resale value of your home may go down if the conservatory is not in keeping with the design of the property, you have shrunk your garden dramatically to accommodate it, or its inadequate heating and ventilation make it too cold in winter or too hot in summer.

Bear in mind that a conservatory built where it is sunniest will result in a magnification of light and heat where it is least needed. A north-facing conservatory brings in light to a dark area and a comfortable level of warmth.

CONVERTING A BASEMENT

Basements, once thought only good enough to store coal or junk, are making a comeback. This is in response to changing lifestyles and soaring land values.

A good conversion can transform a basement into a family room, playroom, gym, sauna, library, wine cellar or snooker room. They can provide accommodation for au pairs or nannies or even be used as swimming pools. An increasing number of people working at home are using their basements as offices. And a basement used as a self-contained flat can recoup its costs in a few years if rented out.

Building organisations including the British Cement Association, the National House Building Council and the Building Research Establishment set up the Basement Development Group in 1992 because of increasing interest in basement building. Their engineers, surveyors, scientists and other representatives advise developers unsure of the building techniques basements require.

Basements are quiet because they're in the ground and typically have a concrete floor. They're thermally more efficient as they're insulated. They produce a more stable building as the foundations go deeper. They're environmentally friendly as they maximise landspace.

Modern basements need to have natural daylight. People tend to associate them with cellars, but now light wells can be dropped down.

But converting an existing cellar or creating a basement in an existing house are also increasingly popular choices. Many homeowners requiring relatively inexpensive extra living space because of, for example, a change in circumstances such as the arrival of a new baby, the need to work from home or teenagers wanting more room, are having their sights set downwards rather than opting for an extension or a house move.

Using a specialised contractor, it can cost from just £10,000 to convert a damp, dark, small cellar into a bright living space. A cellar conversion encompassing the whole basement floor, damp-proofing or 'tanking' the outer walls with a waterproof membrane and knocking out interior walls to open out the space, may cost £50,000 or more.

LOFT CONVERSIONS

While moving house to gain a study, playroom, or an extra bedroom can be very expensive and cause loads of disruption, a loft conversion is typically a fraction of the cost.

Yet the complex building and planning regulations can mean that design-wise you won't necessarily get what you first envisaged and it may cost far more than you bargained for to make the alteration to your house completely safe and legal.

Some people are tempted to try to do a loft conversion on the cheap, ignoring the regulations, but the end result could be a room that is boiling in summer and freezing in winter, a dangerous structure and a fire hazard, and could cause real headaches when it comes to sell as surveyors look to see whether a conversion has been approved by the council. To make things worse, the costs of putting things right could mean you pay twice over or are forced to decrease the selling price.

The financial benefits of a loft conversion can vary enormously depending on where you live. Although a well-designed one can add a substantial amount to the value of a property in an area where space is scarce and house prices are rising, if local house prices are low and static, don't assume you'll recoup the building costs when you come to sell.

A staircase and adequate doorway are crucial for a loft conversion: if there is only a pull-up ladder, or the doorway is not full height, you cannot later put the home on the market describing it as having an extra bedroom.

Loft conversions are a particularly green way to create more living space. You can gain up to 30 per cent extra living space without eating up garden space as you would with a costly extension.

A loft conversion also gives your home the flexibility to adapt to your changing needs as your life unfolds. It might change in use from storage area to bedroom, as a young couple begin a family, then as time goes on become a teenage den and back to a bedroom again as space is made elsewhere in the house for elderly relatives to move in. Increasingly, lofts are being turned in to studies as more and more people work from home.

Though far more professional than sketching out a loft conversion plan on a scrap of paper and then enlisting a mate and a DIY book to do the work, use of a builder, architect and structural engineer can be a costly route to creating your new room in the attic. The Yellow Pages lists many companies who specialise in loft conversions and which can offer a complete, competitive package, often at a lower price.

The first step to a loft conversion is to see whether your roof is suitable for conversion. Is there decent height – about 2.3 metres extending over 50 per cent of the floor area? You will have to check with your local planning department to see whether planning permission is required. You or your builder or architect will have to lodge an application under building regulations with your local authority, and submit detailed plans and structural design calculations.

Get several quotes as they can vary widely in this competitive industry. See examples of completed work before you commit yourself to a contract.

WORKING FROM HOME

More and more people are working from home, yet if you are to become a homeworker it is vital to arrange your living space so that you have minimal distractions and can separate your work from the rest of your life. Many people who don't create a distinct, separate working area complain that work and home life merge so much that they never 'switch off', or that the disruption caused by working at the kitchen table is very counterproductive.

The commonest solution is to convert a spare bedroom into an office. If you have a big enough garden it is surprisingly cheap to create a separate home office by installing a quick-to-assemble timber lodge which comes complete with electricity, plumbing, carpeting and double glazing. These range from around £8,000 to over £30,000 including installation and planning permission is seldom required as such structures are not permanent, but always check with your local planning department.

Help is at hand if you are a homeworker with no budget or plans to move, yet are already too cramped to work effectively. Specialist companies, like Sharps Home Office, can design and install a customised unobtrusive office in the corner of a room that makes the best use of every inch. Good home office furniture is available from suppliers that include IKEA, Just Desks and Spacemaker. Neville Johnson specialise in making home offices for awkward areas such as attics, basements or under the stairs.

It is important to inform your insurance company that you are working from home as your household insurance could be invalid if you work in a home insured only for residential use. Some standard contents insurance policies cover business equipment, such as a computer or fax machine, but further cover may be necessary.

If clients or colleagues are likely to visit, third party liability insurance would cover you against a claim made against you if a visitor was injured at your home.

Your mortgage lender may need to be informed if you work from home, and if your property is rented or leased there may be a clause in the letting agreement excluding such activities. Computer work is unlikely to be a problem, but if the property has to be altered, its value could be affected.

You should also check with your local authority, even if you don't need planning permission. Rooms used for work could be liable for business rates, but your council tax bill should therefore be reduced.

Your local tax office will be able to advise about the household costs (such as a proportion of the heating bill) you can offset against tax, and also any capital gains tax liabilities working from home may incur.

Check your deeds for the property for conditions barring commercial activities in your home.

Members of the Telework, Telecottage and Telecentre Association benefit from publications, an advice line, seminars and discounts on events, equipment and services.

USEFUL TELEPHONE NUMBERS/ EMAIL ADDRESSES

FINDING A BUILDER

London Women and Manual Trades: 020 7251 9192; Quality Mark Scheme hotline: 0845 300 8040; The Stationery Office: 0870 600 5522.

GAS

Transco: 0800 111999 (24-hour helpline); 0800 371782 (for list of emergency contractors).

ELECTRICITY

24Seven: 0800 028 0247

TENNIS COURTS

Specialist tennis court installers include Cambridge Courts, 01638 731400; Doe Sport Ltd, 01277 899333; S.S.G. Landscape Construction, 01245 231777.

SWIMMING POOLS

Jetstream: 0117 938 2515; Lanzare: 01865 883727; Pool Industry Promotion: 01753 621277; SPATA: 01264 356210.

Swimming pool stockists include: Simplex Pools, 01243 781135; Aqua Pools, 01263 833847; Seymour Swimming Pools, 01555 666123; Chiswell Pools, 01923 269822; Colvic Craft (fibreglass pools), 01787 223993.

TIPS FOR ENERGY EFFICIENCY

Energy Advice Centre: 0800 512012

SOLAR POWER

Solar Design Company: 0151 606 0207; Wind and Sun: 01568 760671.

FIREPLACES

Diligence Fires, 01264 811660; Amazing Grates, 020 8883 5556; The Platonic Fireplace Company, 020 8891 5904; The Ceramic Stove Company, 01865 245077.

REDUCING ALLERGENS AND CHEMICAL IRRITANTS IN YOUR HOME

A good range of anti-allergy products are available from the Healthy House, 01453 752216. Low allergy carpeting is available from Kingsmead Carpets, 01290 421 5111 and paints from Lakeland Paints, 01539 732866. Medivac, 01625 539401, can supply suitable bedding.

The National Asthma Campaign, 0845 7010203, the British Allergy Foundation, 020 8303 8583 and the Department of the Environment air pollution information service, 0800 556677 can all provide free advice, and a free leaflet, *Good Air Quality in Your Home* is available from the Department of the Environment, 0870 122 6236.

CABINS AND LODGES

Norwegian Log Chalets, 01189 662146; Homelodge Buildings, 01962 881480; Log Chalet and Pool Co, 01737 241109.

WORKING FROM HOME

IKEA, 020 8208 5601; Just Desks, 020 7723 7976; Neville Johnson, 0161 873 8333; Sharps Home Office, 0800 323232; Spacemaker, 01268 472020; Telework, Telecottage and Telecentre Association, 0800 616008.

10 RAISING CASH FROM YOUR HOME

You can use your home to raise money in a variety of ways, although it is wise to resist for as long as possible anything that reduces your equity in the property (remortgaging in order to take out a bigger loan, for example) as it is all too easy to overborrow and greatly increase your financial risk.

REMORTGAGING

That said, financial experts regularly express their astonishment that few homeowners regularly remortgage, to take advantage of better deals. A new mortgage for the same amount offering just a small reduction in the interest rate can make substantial savings to the monthly mortgage payments, and easily offset the costs and time spent switching deals.

FLEXIBLE MORTGAGES

Effortless equity release only when you need it is available from the growing range of flexible mortgages, which, when used efficiently, can slash substantial sums from the total amount paid during the life of the loan.

When considering a flexible mortgage ask the lender whether you can take a payments break if you need to, for example, because of unemployment or a career break. How easy is it to draw on extra funds and how much can you obtain? Can you make regular overpayments of any size? Are there early redemption penalties? What are the set-up fees? Are there safeguards against overborrowing and risking getting into negative equity? There is more on flexible mortgages in Chapter 6.

EQUITY RELEASE SCHEMES

Older homeowners (generally over sixty) can ask their financial adviser about equity release schemes, which allow capital to be released or income earned from their homes. Although such schemes have had a bad press in the past, they have much improved in recent years. They consist of:

- *home income plans*: you take out a loan and use the money to buy an annuity which provides an income for life. The fixed interest on the loan is paid out of the income from the annuity
- *home reversion plans*: you sell part of the value of your property in return for an income for life. You can instead raise a lump sum and have the right to remain in the home as a tenant for life
- *cash release schemes*: becoming more popular and allow you to borrow a fixed percentage of the value of the home and to spend or invest
- *fixed appreciation mortgages*: involve taking out a loan to buy an annuity
- *shared appreciation mortgages:* allow you to take a cash loan if you agree to let the lender take a share of the future appreciation in the value of the home. The loan is repaid when you die, or the property is sold.

Help the Aged (020 7278 1114) has a booklet on the subject entitled *Capital Release Plans*.

BUY-TO-LET

Many homeowners remortgage their homes to raise the deposit for a further property or further properties to rent out bought as an investment through a buy-to-let loan. The money to pay off the buy-to-let mortgage is raised from the rent tenants pay on the rented property.

LET-TO-BUY

Another option is to do the reverse of buying to let: letting to buy. The first step is to move out of your home into a rented property. You then let out your home, using the rent you receive to cover the mortgage and upkeep, and then take out a buy-to-let loan to buy a new home. If your old property rises in value, or if you sell it within three years of moving out, you would be exempt from paying any capital gains tax.

START UP A BUSINESS

You can use equity in your home for a remortgage or second mortgage to finance the start up of a new business. Yet this can be risky as nearly half start-up businesses cease trading after three years. If the business flops, you could risk losing your home.

YOUR PROPERTY AS A TV/FILM/PHOTOGRAPHIC LOCATION

When people talk about locations for film and TV, it usually evokes images of Merchant–Ivory films, Hollywood blockbusters or BBC costume dramas. But advertising and fashion shoots and day-to-day TV programmes using less grand properties, bring in much of the income.

The demand for people's homes as locations is so great that there are a number of location libraries and agencies specialising in finding the right properties, such as Amazing Space. The London Film Commission also sources locations.

What such agencies look for in each property is a good example of its type, whether it's a tower-block council house or grand mansion, to have character and individuality or have special features such as a spiral staircase or interesting doors and windows. And they are continually looking for something new.

Don't just think of the front of your house. You may have something unusual like an amazing tiled bathroom. The property should be light, and spacious enough to fit a crew although space is not so crucial for still photo shoots.

Fees paid by production companies vary greatly, typically anything from £200 to over £5,000 a day. Shoots can last from a single day or for several months. Fees generally increase in proportion to the amount of disruption experienced.

Most shoots involve at least a dozen people, so you need to be relaxed and flexible. Serious damage to property is extremely rare, but it is important to draw up a contract to cover all eventualities. Avoid like the plague agencies that ask for a fee to go on their books.

LAND TO BUILD ON

If you have a garden that is bigger than you need, you could consider applying for planning permission to build on it and sell the land to a developer. Your neighbours may not be particularly grateful, though.

RENT YOUR ROOF TO A TELECOMMUNICATIONS COMPANY

There's ongoing controversy over whether mobile telephone antennae, masts and aerials are a health risk because of the radiation they emit, and their installation often causes fierce opposition in the locality. But if this does not worry you, it may be possible to have one of these installed on your roof. The average rental telecommunications companies currently pay for such 'macrocell' installations is £9,200 per year. Nabarro Nathanson has a free leaflet on the subject, *Rooftop Rents*.

LETTING AND LODGERS

Renting out a room in your home or your whole home on a long-term or short-term basis, is often financially rewarding. The different options are explored in the Letting section of this chapter.

A FEW WORDS OF WARNING

Remember that if you want to raise cash from your home, house prices can fall as well as rise, and repeated borrowing increases the risk. Treat borrowing against your home as a temporary measure, and reduce the debt as soon as possible by making higher repayments.

Elderly people should take independent advice before considering an equity release scheme, and avoid any loan that does not have a fixed rate. Second mortgages are to be avoided as the borrowing rate will be high, and you could lose your home if you get behind with payments.

Also, remember that if you trade down in the property market you may not be able to trade up again. If you move out of London, in particular, it may be impossible to get back on the property ladder in the capital.

LETTING

RENTING OUT A ROOM

If you are struggling with mortgage payments or just need some extra cash, letting a spare room can be a good way to boost income, and the first £4,250 of rent paid each year (£81.73 per week) is tax free under the government's rent-a-room scheme.

Under the terms of a residential mortgage you are required to inform your lender that you are doing this. Usually your mortgage will not be changed as the property remains your home rather than a second property. If you decide to move out, you may have to switch to a more expensive buy-to-let mortgage.

Lodgers have no legal rights when they occupy your home, and therefore there aren't potential problems with them becoming sitting tenants. A weekly or monthly let, otherwise known as a 'periodic tenancy', is the most flexible option for both landlord and tenant and allows both parties to end the tenancy at short notice.

Taking in a lodger can also provide companionship. Select the right individuals and you might be lucky enough to have a real-life *Friends* on your hands – sparkling people who love each other and never argue about the washing up. But get it wrong and the classic lodgers' sitcom, *Rising Damp*, will look like paradise.

Sharing your home with a lodger is quite an intimate kind of relationship. It can have some of the features of marriage and your life isn't always your own. If you don't set down your conditions of the rental at the outset, you could find yourself dealing with such problems as excessive noise, an unwelcome influx of visitors, smoking you out with a fifty-a-day fag habit or non-payment of rent.

Answer your tenant's questions before he or she asks them. Which rooms does he or she have access to? Will you provide meals or cleaning supplies? How much rent and deposit do you want in advance? Do you mind noise after 10 p.m.? Are smokers, pets or overnight visitors allowed? Establish rules for washing up, cooking, buying food or use of the phone.

It's important to interview prospective tenants very carefully. Put them on a week's notice and a week's trial. It's tempting to not bother to check references, but it could save much difficulty in the future. Make sure they're reliable references, such as their bank manager or their employer, or their college if they are a student. It's no good ringing their mate who'd happily swear a convicted armed bank robber was a member of the clergy.

A written tenancy agreement can save on acrimony and frustration in the long run. The agreement doesn't have to be drawn up by a solicitor, but as taking on a lodger is quite a major step, it's worthwhile.

One thing to consider very carefully is taking in a friend as a lodger, because when you live with a friend, often the first thing that strains is the friendship itself. Especially when you find the charming wit you used to enjoy seeing at the club swiftly changes into a miserable, inconsiderate manic depressive whose only callers are bailiffs.

If you're single, think twice about letting a couple share with you. They may take the place over. Because it's two against one they'll always win in any disagreement.

To calculate what constitutes a fair rent, look at the adverts in newsagents' windows or the local press. Decide exactly what you will charge for. Will you charge extra for bills or include them in the rent? Tenants will expect a furnished bedroom with access to a kitchen, bathroom and living room at the very least.

If your property is leasehold, check whether there are any restrictions, and ask your insurance company whether your housing insurance would be affected. Ask them how they would deal with a claim for damage incurred by a lodger.

If, despite all your preparations you are not happy with your lodger, the 1988 Housing Act has simplified eviction. If the tenant lives with you and has shared use of accommodation such as kitchen and bathroom, you do not need to obtain a court order. You still have to give them notice because you've entered into a contract. If a week's rent has been payable in advance, a week's notice may be reasonable. If they still haven't gone after that, you can peacefully enter their room. Wait until they go out, carefully pack their stuff for later collection and change the locks.

If they have self-contained facilities you'd need to get a court order, giving a minimum of four weeks' notice. Court costs could be in excess of £500.

Before advertising for your first tenant ensure that all services, such as heating, lighting and plumbing, are in good working order, attend to anything that needs repair and give the property a thorough clean, repainting where necessary. Pack away anything sentimentally or otherwise valuable.

As well as advertising privately in newspapers or on a website, you could register with a lettings agent. Select one that is a member of the Association of Residential Letting Agents or other similar recognised body. Typically, agents charge around 10 per cent of annual income to secure a tenant and an extra 5 per cent for managing the property.

The agent should provide an *assured short-hold tenancy agreement* typically lasting six or twelve months for both parties to sign. This gives the landlord a guaranteed right to repossess the property after the period of tenancy has expired. Some tenants request an *assured tenancy,* which provides the tenant with the right to stay at the property as long as the landlord is unable to provide a valid reason to gain possession.

You should provide a full inventory down to the last teaspoon and it is a good idea to take pictures of the property. Unlike in the past, there is no difference legally whether the property is furnished or unfurnished.

LONG-TERM LETTING

There are plenty of reasons you might want to let out your home for a few months or years. If your job causes you to relocate for a couple of years, or you fancy sailing around the world for six months or you've slipped into negative equity, or are struggling with the mortgage and one solution would be to rent out your home and move into somewhere cheaper for a year, a long let may be ideal.

To start with, ask two or three letting agents that are members of the Association of Residential Letting Agents to assess the property. Before tenants move in, shut away or sort out storage for things that are particularly valuable for either emotional or financial reasons. Clear out cupboards and bookcases and remove ornaments and other personal things so that your tenants have a chance to put their stamp on your property for the time they will be there. Sort out adequate insurance, explaining to your insurer the new circumstances.

It is no wonder that buying property to let out has become so popular as a form of investment in recent years. If it goes well, you get to create income from the monthly rental, and at the same time your property is rising in value.

Yet, there are numerous potential pitfalls. For example, the recent popularity of buy-to-let mortgages resulted in too many properties available for rent in many areas and made letting more difficult generally.

IS LETTING FOR YOU?

Becoming a landlord can involve a lot of work: compiling an inventory, complying with fire and safety regulations, sourcing and checking a suitable tenancy agreement, informing utility companies of new tenants and repairs and maintenance, just for starters. You may have to deal with lettings agents, solicitors, local boroughs, accountants, the Inland Revenue – and the county court if there are problems.

If the property is leasehold, there may be a managing agent, the freeholder and a residents' association to deal with. You may have to deal with void periods when the property seems permanently unrentable, or tenants who hold regular parties that keep the neighbours up on a weekly basis, who let the bath flood the flat downstairs and who are never contactable when you want to discuss the mounting rent arrears.

THE RIGHT PROPERTY

A successful landlord requires an ability to spot a property that will let well. Such a property will typically be decorated in neutral colours, be clean and well maintained and have a spotless kitchen and bathroom. It will be very near public transport and shops and other facilities. Tenants are generally after convenience rather than things like a garden or garage.

Little touches like installing a house plant in the corner of the room or slinging out an ugly sofa for an attractive contemporary model can make all the difference.

Studios and small flats are usually the easiest to let, and the bigger the property, the more difficult it can be to find a tenant. It's vital to research the area, for one full of families who mostly own their homes is likely to have considerably less letting potential than an area chock-full of employment opportunities and lots of rented property.

FINDING A TENANT

If you do the searching yourself, you will have to pay for advertising in newspapers as well as spend time showing prospective tenants around and checking out their references, which should be from their bank, previous landlord and current employer.

Taylor Trent Management offers a referencing package to landlords for £23.50. The Tenancy Information Centre, through the Small Landlord's Association, can check to see whether your prospective tenant has defaulted on rental payments in the past.

As well as taking the standard one month's rent and one month's deposit in advance, you should obtain an assured Short-hold tenancy agreement from a stationer to ensure your legal safeguards.

LETTINGS AGENCIES

Agencies typically charge 10 per cent of the rent for the whole tenancy for finding the tenant, which is payable at the start of the tenancy. The commission rate generally reduces the longer the tenant stays, so it may go down to 7.5 per cent in year two and 5 per cent in year three. The agency should make all the necessary checks for you and provide the assured Short-hold tenancy agreement, but they are no guarantee against finding yourself with a bad tenant.

Fees generally increase if the let is short term or if there are extra responsibilities, such as collecting the rent and attending to repairs and renovation.

Choose an agency that is a member of a professional body such as the Association of Residential Letting Agents (A.R.L.A.), which must satisfy its requirements, which include the need for suitable professional indemnity insurance. A.R.L.A. can provide free literature about letting. The National Association of Estate Agents (N.A.E.A.) is another option. The National Approved Lettings Scheme (Nals) has set a minimum standard of service for lettings agents to adhere to.

What are your first impressions of the agent? Are the phones answered efficiently? Do they return calls? Do they arrive on time for your valuation? Do they have a nearby office and act on behalf of other local property? Would their tenants suit your property and budget? When are they open? Not all tenants can view between nine and five. Don't be afraid to instruct two or three agents, to get a wider coverage.

An increasing number of Internet letting agencies are appearing (for example, **www.holiday-rentals.co.uk**) and here, typically, rather than agency fees to pay, you only pay for use of the website, at around £150 a year.

THE PROPERTY

Ensure there are clear instructions for appliances, plenty of information about things like rubbish collection and using the burglar alarm and contact details for things like doctors, dentists, hospitals, emergency plumbers and electricians. The tenancy will start off on a better footing if you include details of local restaurants, shops and places of interest, and maybe a welcoming pack of bread, milk, fruit and a bottle of wine.

Never enter the premises without permission from your tenant as it is their home while the tenancy agreement is running. Be fair about returning the deposit at the end of the tenancy. If it is in the same good condition as it should have been when the tenant moved in, return the deposit promptly as it may be needed for the tenant's next home.

TAX

If you receive income from a property you need to complete the relevant land and property pages on your tax return and submit it to the Inland Revenue by each 31 January.

Against your income from renting out property you can deduct expenses such as the interest (rather than capital repayment) payments on your mortgage, advertising, council tax, buildings and contents insurance and insurance against non-payment of rent and travelling costs related to visiting the property.

General information on letting is available from Leaders (**www.leaders.co.uk**). The Office of the Deputy Prime Minister's website has information concerning letting rooms and rights to security of tenure. Contact your local county court to obtain publications concerning assured tenancies and gaining possession.

SHORT LETS

An increasing number of homeowners are renting out their properties for as little as a few days at a time, an ideal option for when you go on holiday. Choose a reputable agent to find reliable tenants and not only do you receive an appreciable sum for the days you're away, but your short-term tenants protect against burglars too.

Short lets are popular with an increasing band of business and holiday travellers who dislike the anonymity and restrictions of a hotel or corporate flat. They opt to stay in private properties for the privacy, greater comfort, better value and personal touch a private home can offer.

Short lets have come into their own since the Rent Act was changed in 1993, protecting landlords from sitting tenants. There's no security of tenure if they pay in advance and have arrival and departure dates. You get paid the full rent in advance and don't have the threat of being landed with a sitting tenant.

Letting your home for just a week or two each year can be highly lucrative, usually substantially more than you'd receive per week for a long-term let.

Homes do not need to be immaculate to be suitable for short-term lets. All that clients require is a clean, well-decorated, uncluttered home in good condition with a modern kitchen and bathroom. Neutral colours are best – the simpler the decor the better.

The legal and financial implications of letting your home for short periods are relatively simple. A legally binding holiday letting booking form and invoice take care of the legal side, unlike for longer lets, over a matter of months, where you should use a tenancy agreement.

Unlike a long let, the owner pays all bills except the phone and provides everything a tenant would need, from linen and towels to a video recorder.

There are income tax implications, but mortgage interest, agent's fees (typically 10–15 per cent), repair and maintenance costs, water and insurance rates can be deducted from rental income.

Agents usually take a deposit from tenants, but owners are responsible for insuring their belongings, and normal household insurance policies can be affected by short lets. If you have a leasehold property, check you are not contravening the lease by embarking upon a short let. Check with your tax office about the tax obligations, although expenses like agent's fees, insurance, repair and maintenance costs, can all be deducted from rental income.

Sporting and cultural events increase opportunities for short lets. The tennis championships at Wimbledon are a great money-spinner with the media as well as players to house, but many homeowners let out their homes during other events such as the

Chelsea Flower Show, Henley Regatta, and the Edinburgh, Ross-on-Wye and Glyndebourne Festivals. The six-month polo season around Cirencester and homes near Ascot, Aintree, Goodwood and York racecourses are popular.

Many letting agencies will say that administrative costs will be too high to justify a short let, so go to a specialist short or holiday letting agency.

BUY-TO-LET

Jumping on the buy-to-let bandwagon – where you buy and rent out a home with the mortgage paid by the rental income – has become something of a roller-coaster ride of late.

Buy-to-let mortgages were devised and launched in 1996 by the Association of Residential Letting Agents and have been a huge success, creating a whole new generation of amateur part-time landlords. Many borrowers have made great financial gains on their properties and don't regret their actions a bit.

But, as there's no mercy shown to amateurs in business, a substantial number have had their fingers burnt. If property values come crashing down or interest rates soar, or it gets increasingly difficult to find tenants, the financial future for many more such people may become very rocky.

The rise in the number of rental properties available has given tenants more choice, and cheaper and cheaper mortgage deals lead tenants to buy properties themselves rather than continue to rent, resulting in difficulties for landlords to find new tenants. Yet if you take the long-term view and select your property carefully, the scheme can result in an excellent investment.

A salary deemed too small for a conventional mortgage of the same size doesn't necessarily have to prevent a person getting a buy-to-let mortgage as the amount you can borrow on such a mortgage is, on the whole, based on the amount of rental income it is projected you will receive rather than on salary.

You typically have to pay a deposit on a buy-to-let mortgage, as little as 10 per cent, but usually 15 or 20 per cent, and many buyers raise this on remortgaging their current home. If all the figures add up satisfactorily in the lender's view, you can borrow a surprisingly high amount.

For example, if your current home has increased in value by £50,000 since you bought it, even if your salary hasn't increased, you could in theory in some cases use the £50,000 to pay deposits to buy one or even several homes you plan to rent out, assuming it's reckoned by the valuer that the rent received will cover the mortgage payments and a bit extra and you fulfil the lender's other lending criteria.

To maximise your chances of buying a successful buy-to-let property, the most important factor to consider is location. Buying close to train and underground stations and good local amenities like shops, restaurants, bars, cinemas and clubs obviously greatly increases the attraction of your property to a prospective tenant in the town, while an attractive property set amidst beautiful countryside and situated away from industry is ideal for a rural purchase.

The type of property is important: one- and two-bed flats are easiest to let, in a well-maintained building in a pleasant, quiet street. Today's tenants increasingly demand properties that are well-equipped and furnished, with facilities like a microwave, dishwasher and washer-dryer, although more and more are requesting homes that are unfurnished.

Generally, smaller, cheaper homes provide better yields – the yearly rent as a proportion of the value of the home – so a £50,000 flat is likely to be a better earner proportionally than a house at ten times its value, although it is unlikely to rise proportionally as greatly in value in the long term.

Homes in new developments are always popular with tenants, being bright, clean and boasting the latest housing designs. High specifications like fully fitted kitchens and a pristine decorative finish ensure low-maintenance living for both landlord and tenant.

With buy-to-let, it is better to invest in two cheaper properties rather than one expensive one to spread the risk and maximise returns. Be prepared to invest in the property for at least ten years to ride out any financial storms. Be prepared for falling rents, bad tenants and void periods (no tenants). You may get high rental income or good capital growth but rarely both.

Research your location well: generally you'll get the highest rental income from cheaper properties in university towns and cities and the highest capital appreciation from upmarket city homes. Renters like neutrally decorated properties close to public transport and amenities like schools. Remember the fees, both for purchasing the property plus letting/management fees, service charges, council tax, insurance, maintenance and so forth.

LET-TO-BUY

Another option is to do the reverse of buying to let: letting to buy. The first step is to move out of your home into a rented property. You then let out your home, using the rent you receive to cover the mortgage and upkeep, and then take out a buy-to-let loan to buy a new home. If your old property rises in value, if you sell it within three years of moving out you would be exempt from paying any capital gains tax.

Let-to-buy can also be an ideal solution for someone relocating for, say, a couple of years who wants to keep their present home.

USEFUL TELEPHONE NUMBERS/ EMAIL ADDRESSES

EQUITY RELEASE SCHEMES

Help the Aged: 020 7278 1114

YOUR PROPERTY AS A TV/FILM/PHOTOGRAPHIC LOCATION

Amazing Space, 020 7729 0919; London Film Commission, 020 7387 8787.

RENT YOUR ROOF TO A TELECOMMUNICATIONS COMPANY

Nabarro Nathanson: 020 7524 6000.

LETTING

Leaders, Osprey House, 16–18 Worthing Road, Horsham, Sussex RH12 1SL, 01403 249200; Taylor Trent Management, 01476 514695.

SHORT LETS

Home from Home, 020 7584 8914; A Place Like Home, 020 7228 4668; Mackays Agency, 0131 225 3539; Country Chapters, 020 7722 0722; Go Native, 020 7286 1088; In The English Manner, 0155 937 1600; International Chapters, 020 7722 0722.

11 SELLING YOUR HOME

THE COST OF SELLING

A £100,000 house typically costs around £2,400 to sell, based on an estate agent taking a 2 per cent commission (£2,000) and conveyancing costs of around £400. Sometimes there are estate agent's advertising fees to pay as well, which may be several hundred pounds. Removal, redecorating and other relocation costs are likely to add at least an extra 3 or 4 per cent or so of the value of the property to the final bill.

SELLERS' PACKS

If you want to sell your home, is it right that you be forced to part with an up-front fee of around £300 to £1,000 to market it? That is what the government plans to introduce – a nationwide compulsory sellers' pack, in a bid to speed up and simplify the homebuying process and eliminate gazumping (where a second buyer offers a higher price after a sale has been agreed). It is estimated that this new scheme will cost homeowners around £700 million a year. Those that don't comply could be fined up to £5,000 if a pack is not produced within fourteen days and if this is ignored, prison sentences are possible.

The sellers' packs will contain a house condition (survey) report, replies to local authority searches, title/ownership documents, replies to buyers' standard enquiries, copies of planning, building regulations and listed building approvals and consents, warranties for newly built homes, guarantees for any work carried out and a draft contract.

Packs for leasehold properties will also require details of the lease, service charge details, the buildings insurance policy and any regulations made by the landlord.

Having a survey and documentation made available in advance should mean that the time between the offer and exchange will be reduced, lessening the chance of sales falling through.

But owners of cheaper properties will certainly feel the pinch if they are forced to spend from several hundred pounds just to join the housing market, with no refund if they then decide to take their home off the market if it is less favourable than they were expecting.

There has been criticism that the pack's house condition report, something between a mortgage company's valuation and a home buyer's report, may not be detailed enough. In a market when homes are slow to shift it could easily become outdated, and how many buyers will necessarily trust a survey prepared on behalf of a desperate seller or seller commissioning the cheapest surveyor to cut costs? Many will continue to commission their own full structural surveys and be obliged to pay for a valuation report to satisfy their lender.

The scheme does not address the issue of commitment, the enemy of gazumping. Buyers and sellers can still walk away from the deal after agreeing a sale. With this scheme, nothing is binding until contracts are exchanged. The current normal procedure for buying a home in Scotland, by contrast, is to bid for a home and if your offer is agreed you are locked into a legally binding contract. It's a pity the sellers' pack does not include a legally binding contract pledging that both parties keep to the offered price.

TAX IMPLICATIONS OF SELLING

Capital gains tax can be payable on your property when you sell if it is not your main home or if you have used it as a place of business where you have claimed expenses. The tax is payable on the net profit of the sale of the relevant portion of the property (a study used for your business, for example) minus the cost of improvements and the cost of buying and selling.

WHEN TO SELL

There are too many factors at work in the sale of a property to give a definitive answer to this, but if you are a vendor, it is probably best to follow the pack: the best time to sell is likely to be when the majority of other sellers are trying to, in the spring. The surge in activity almost always causes prices to rise and some buyers to panic, believing that if they don't make a quick decision to buy, the best homes will either sell to someone else or rise in price.

There tends to be an influx of enquiries in the new year, as people have decided to move in the coming year, but it doesn't tend to translate into sales until later.

Contrary to popular belief, on bank holidays and during all school holidays, including half terms, agents see a clear drop in activity rather than busier times as people increasingly protect their precious leisure time. This can translate into some prices dropping as properties fail to budge.

Not only does the bad weather of winter discourage many buyers from searching for a home, but vendors know that their home is likely to be looking increasingly less attractive than in the spring and summer. Things are quietest in December, as both buyers and sellers turn their attentions and budgets to Christmas.

The market is slightly boosted from the spring onwards by buyers relocating for their childrens' new schools in preparation for the new educational year in September. The payment of very generous city bonuses in the early months of each year to the city and financial sectors can have a surprising effect on the upper end of the housing market in the south-east, which in turn can stimulate activity further down the housing ladder. Not just senior staff receive them: thousands of support staff like secretaries and computer personnel can receive big awards too.

HIRING AN ESTATE AGENT

Despite the negative view so many people have of estate agents, the overwhelming majority of buyers and sellers still use them.

Understandably, many estate agents feel they do a lot more than simply wait for a few prospective buyers to appear, show some people around the odd house and then help themselves to a few thousand pounds. They feel that the no sale, no fee system couldn't be fairer, that they help in other ways, such as advising upon mortgage restrictions, and that being open six or seven days a week means few enquiries are missed.

About 90 per cent of house sales are through estate agents, and their commission rates in the UK are amongst the cheapest in the world. Estate agents liase with other agents when there's a chain, and check the suitability of prospective buyers. An agent's expertise can usually get the vendor a better price that more than compensates for the commission charged.

The National Association of Estate Agents believes that the 'cowboy' element of estate agency has all but disappeared, because in recent years agents have had to comply with legislation such as the Property Misdescriptions Act and the Trades Descriptions Act.

Even so, take time to find the agent or agents to use. Some may specialise in expensive homes, others may consistently deal with the cheapest ones, or properties in need of modernisation.

Their fees typically range from 1.5 per cent to 4 per cent of the asking price plus VAT currently 17.5 per cent. This may sound like a lot but it can be substantially more on the Continent and in America.

You can take on an agent on a sole retained basis, where only that firm will be dealing with your sale. This should be at a lower rate than if you sell using more than one estate agency. High commissions are often negotiable – get the agreed rate in writing.

When choosing an agent, find out their knowledge of the area and see what other types of property they have on their books.

GETTING THE BEST FROM YOUR ESTATE AGENT

Many people are suspicious of estate agents, who can't win either way. If they sell your property in a day, you begrudge giving them a seemingly huge sum for their efforts. If they take months to sell they are deemed incompetent and therefore don't deserve their fee.

Yet selling your property quickly may be due to their contacts and experience, and a slow seller may be due to factors out of their control.

Anyone can set up in business selling property, so check that the agent or agents you are dealing with belong to a professional body such as the National Association of Estate Agents. Some agents may be members of the Royal Institution of Chartered Surveyors, the Architects and Surveyors Institute or the Association of Building Engineers.

Use an agent who knows the area and local market well. The more property the agent has sold in the street the better. See how much business they're doing in the area. Ask a lot of questions. Experience counts a lot. You want an agent who can successfully combine assessing what's been selling recently, seeing where the market is now, and reading into how the market will be over the next few months when the property will be on the market.

Agents are used to haggling. Using one could cost 2 per cent in a city centre, sometimes 3 per cent, and nearer 1.5 per cent where property prices are low. Some agents will agree to a sliding scale, for example, 2 per cent if they sell at the asking price and 2.5 per cent if they sell it for £5,000 more. Yet asking to pay a lower fee can demoralise the agent and it can be more effective to offer an incentive, such as a bonus if the property sells above the agreed price or faster than expected.

Check in advance what is included in the package. Do you have to pay extra for a 'for sale board', advertisements in property magazines or the local press or a glossy brochure?

Ask the agency to confirm its fees and what will be included in writing. You will be given an agreement to sign. Carefully look at the clauses. Avoid committing yourself to a lengthy sole agency contract. If you are not happy with the agent a few weeks down the line, you want to be able to terminate the agreement quickly.

You don't want to be in the position where you are liable to pay commission if your plans change or a problem comes up and you are unable to sell to the buyer the agent has introduced. Some clauses commit you to paying the agent commission for introducing the buyer whether the sale goes ahead or not.

Beware of sole selling rights. This entitles the agent to a commission even if you sell the house yourself, such as to a friend.

Ensure the photographs of your property are in colour and are taken during sunlight, ideally in the summer. Good quality interior shots can also help a lot. Check that the agents' descriptions of the property are accurate, especially room and garden dimensions. Make sure that easily overlooked features that could make your property more attractive are mentioned, such as wall cavity insulation and French windows.

GETTING THE CORRECT VALUATION FOR YOUR PROPERTY

It is curious how people can sell what is usually their biggest asset – their home – at the first or second price they hear.

Valuing property is not an exact science. Agents often come up with wildly differing valuation figures so do not blindly accept what the first one says. Instead, it is important to obtain several valuations from agents, which can vary considerably and which will make little difference to the agent's commission, but could have big financial consequences for you. Ask each one to back up their valuation with an explanation of how they reached that figure.

One problem is that property is so difficult to quantify. It is just an opinion, and is so subjective. A property that you think is great might be thought as dreadful by someone else.

Things like these will bump up the value of a property: easy access to good commuting routes, well sited, such as on the edge of an attractive village, within twenty minutes of a good school, good views, in good structural and decorative order, having extra accommodation such as a self-contained granny flat.

These things will put the price down: a structurally unsound property in poor decorative order, near an industrial/council estate, motorway, railway or aircraft noise, an unattractive view, a large home with inadequate land.

Many factors can affect the price of a home. One house may justify a high price tag because of extensive home improvements, while another may be offered cheaply simply because a quick sale is required due to a bereavement or debt.

For a speedy sale, it's important to have your home priced accurately. Ask too much and you could put off potential buyers, and having to make a price drop a few weeks on could discourage them further. If you have a semi-detached or terraced house similar to others nearby, valuing is simpler as there are other examples for the agent to refer to. But if you have a country or an unusual property, where there's often a lack of direct comparisons, it can be advantageous to pitch a low figure to create interest, allowing competition to increase the price.

You can't agree with your agent on a realistic price to enter the market at unless you are rational about your property in the first place. But most owners look upon their homes far more affectionately than a hard-nosed buyer, who may have traipsed through several similar properties the same day. Try and look at your home from a stranger's point of view, examining its flaws. Next door may have sold recently for more than the amount the agent has valued your home, but maybe it has a better extension, or is decorated to a higher standard.

It can come as quite a surprise to vendors that dropping the asking price of their property is often not as effective as anticipated. Property newly on the market will usually command far more attention from prospective buyers, who often view a home that's been on sale for some months as tarnished.

Bear in mind that there are thousands of agents in Britain chasing a shortage of properties, and so some agents go to great lengths to get your business in the first place. If one values your home at £90,000 and another at £110,000, the one that's wildly off the mark may simply be woefully inexperienced.

But if he's suggested a high figure, he may instead be trying to flatter you to get your business, getting you to bask in the idea of making a handsome profit if you sign up with him, instead of settling for a lower figure with one of his competitors. Of course, being overvalued, the property won't shift in the next few weeks. After a period of inactivity, the agent can then reapproach you and suggest dropping the price to what he knows is a much more realistic figure. By this time you're probably so desperate to sell, you won't think twice about doing so. And it may be difficult to take it off the market if the agent has included a hefty pull-out clause in the contract.

Likewise, you should question the motives of the agent who comes up with the lowest valuation. He may be under pressure to produce a high turnover of sales at his branch. The simplest way to do this is to offer the goods cut-price. It doesn't matter to him – if he sells a property for £100,000 he gets two or three thousand pounds in commission. If he were to sell it at a more realistic £110,000, while the owner may gain nearly £10,000, he's only going to make another couple of hundred pounds or so, and will probably have to wait longer for a sale and therefore wait longer for his money.

There are so many factors that can affect the value of your home. Weighing up the intricate web of pros and cons each property presents can be a complicated affair. Would you rather have a smaller garden that looks out on to an ugly row of shops, or a bigger garden that backs on to a busy main road? It's questions like these that make valuing property so complicated.

Your home will always sell at a premium if it backs on to or is near a river, canal, lake or the sea. Waterfront homes often add around 30 per cent to the value of a home.

The general condition, size or design of extensions or a modern kitchen or bathroom can add or subtract thousands of pounds from the final valuation. Seclusion, mature gardens and selling in the summer all boost a house sale while clutter, a nearby railway line, flight paths, a nearby nightclub or tower block, graffiti or electricity pylons do the opposite. Decorating a property in bright, neutral tones and having paperwork to prove the home has been regularly maintained can boost the price, while a riot of dark brown, purple and orange paint and broken or ill-maintained fittings can help it plummet.

One of the biggest discouraging factors in price is if four-fifths of a house is owner-occupied and a tenant has rights in one room. That would demolish the price.

Schools can affect prices either way. Some buyers will pay substantially over the odds to be in the catchment area of a favoured school, while others will ask for a drop in price if there's a noisy playground at the end of the garden.

Less can mean more. Today's buyer will often be far more impressed by a tastefully restructured home where the bedrooms have been reduced from five cramped boxrooms to three spacious ones if the result is a light and appealing design.

Things that may be very cheap to put right can put off buyers because it can suggest the possibility of more serious problems. A slate missing from the roof could be rectified in five minutes or may be an indication that the whole roof needs replacing. A few suspect cracks in the walls could simply need filling with a dab of plaster, but it may also suggest serious structural problems like subsidence. Many potential buyers don't want to take the risk, or the trouble to find out how serious the problem is. It's well worth looking into the cost of every repair and improvement before putting the property on the market.

Check the Land Registry website (**www.landreg.gov.uk**) and see the prices of what has sold recently nearby.

PRIVATE SALES

It is no surprise that many vendors consider selling their property themselves when they realise the huge cheque they are going to have to hand over to an agent if or when their home shifts.

When a sale goes well an agent can seem invaluable: preparing accurate, effective sales details, looking after all the viewings, weeding out unsuitable buyers and negotiating the best possible price.

Yet many house sales don't go like that, and instead vendors are left to conduct most of the viewings by potential buyers, who have been enticed by inaccurate, imaginative property particulars and who are looking for something completely different, themselves.

In recent years, a number of opportunities have opened up allowing the private individual to market their property inexpensively and easily. But it is best done by those with plenty of time and energy, and good negotiating skills.

The Internet has been the greatest boon for private sales, and a number of sites have opened that allow homeowners to advertise their homes, usually for a small fee. Before approaching one, have your property valued by three or four estate agents first.

Property Broker (**www.propertybroker.com**) is one private sale website, currently covering London and the Home Counties. It charges £97 for a set of digital photographs, a sales board and to post your details on the website, which is linked to other home search sites. For a further fee, it can include property details in its newspaper adverts.

Similar sites include Houseweb (**www.houseweb.co.uk**), which charges from under £50 to about £300 to post details on to the site and provide a board. 4 Sale By Owner (**www.4salebyowner.co.uk**) offers a nationwide service starting at £24.99 for an advertisement with unlimited text and up to four photos. No 1 4 Property (**www.numberone4property.co.uk**) charges £39.95 for up to six photos and a 'For Sale' sign costs an extra £10.

The weekly free-ads publication, *Loot* (**www.loot.com**), is another popular source of privately offered properties. Vendors can pay for its private sale advertising service, which includes a sales board and a prominent ad published for up to twelve weeks. Other outlets for advertising residential property include *Exchange and Mart*, *Daltons Weekly* and the local and national press.

As such services are classed as advertising rather than estate agencies, there should be no problem using them alongside a sole or multiple estate agents – unless the agent has a 'sole selling rights' clause in their contract rather than a 'sole agency' clause. Signing such a clause could mean you having to pay the agent commission even if you sold privately to a friend.

Selling privately is likely to involve more legwork – deciding on an asking price, drawing up particulars, answering enquiries, arranging and carrying out viewings and negotiating. When you find a buyer, the process should then be handed over to your solicitor, who should make sure that the buyer's solicitor sends a formal letter with confirmation of the offer.

As vendors are under no obligation whether they sell privately or through an estate agent, there's little to lose in trying both options. But, if selling privately, ensure sale particulars are accurate, as incorrect statements could result in being sued for damages or cancellation of the contract or both.

SELLING BY HOLDING A COMPETITION

Some vendors have gone to the lengths of holding a competition to sell their homes, for example by organising a raffle and offering the property as the prize. Apart from the terrifying prospect of only managing to sell a fraction of the number of tickets required to raise the current value of your home, holding a raffle or competition could open you to serious legal difficulties and therefore cannot be recommended.

SELLING AT AUCTION

If you sell this way you will be responsible for a number of costs, most significantly the percentage of the auction price payable to the auctioneer, which is commonly around 2.5 per cent.

Selling by auction is particularly suitable if you need to capitalise on the equity in your property quickly, as completion usually takes a maximum of 28 days.

Selling this way can also be the answer if, for whatever reason, your property hasn't sold because of a downturn in the market or some negative aspect the property has, such as subsidence. Equally, in a strong seller's market, you avoid the awkward situation of gazumping.

If you plan to sell by auction, investigate agents and auctioneers carefully and be clear about all costs. Decide on a reserve price (the lowest amount you will accept) and whether you will include a clause ('unless previously sold') allowing you to sell beforehand if a suitable buyer appears.

Appoint a solicitor to deal with prospective buyers before the auction takes place. Having a survey prepared beforehand can facilitate a sale. Bear in mind that the sale is legally binding and if the property fails to reach the reserve price, you will still have to pay the auctioneer.

HOUSE SWAPPING

Swapping rather than selling your home can mean the stamp duty being just £5, and the savings made can be divided between buyer and seller so both parties benefit. The downside to swapping rather than selling your house is the extra difficulty in finding someone happy to make a swap, and also in reaching agreement on the extra amount needed to be paid by one party if one property is worth more than the other, as is likely.

One website, **www.webswappers.com**, has successfully paired up individuals willing to swap their homes. Swappers can place their property swap on the site for free or, for £65, swappers can have a 'For Swap' sign to go outside their home and a digital photograph of the property taken for inclusion on the site.

As an example, if swapping a house worth £350,000 for a house worth £250,000 plus the cash difference of £100,000, special rules for house swapping apply to the cheaper of the two properties as the tax authorities see the transaction as a transfer and the cheaper house is therefore only liable for a £5 fixed duty. The duty is still payable on the more expensive house, but savings can be split between the swappers.

In the above example, buying traditionally rather than swapping, stamp duty at 3 per cent or £7,500 is payable on the £250,000 property and therefore £7,495 is saved.

TIPS FOR SELLING FAST

- **Investigate your buyer: A collapsed sale can waste months and finding out your buyers' circumstances, such as whether they have a mortgage offer, a buyer for their existing property and any potential hurdles to a quick sale, could avoid complications.**
- **Sell to a first-time buyer or a buyer who is not selling: This avoids being caught in a chain of interdependent buyers and sellers.**

Most people make an initial decision whether they might want to buy within the first ten seconds of arriving so making a good first impression is vital when you come to sell. Tidy the garden, sweep the drive, mow the lawn, put up hanging baskets (and remember to water them!), make sure the doorbell works, move the caravan or broken car from the driveway and clean or repaint the windows and front door, polishing any brassware. If you have noisy neighours try to show your home when they are not around (although if you are asked specifically by a prospective buyer whether you have problem neighbours you mustn't lie as there could be a comeback).

Stand outside and look at the house as though you're a buyer. It needs 'kerb appeal'. Ask yourself whether your property looks in tip-top condition.

If you live in a flat make sure the communal areas are looking good. Many fantastic apartments haven't sold because the communal areas were a turn off. Junk the junk mail, sweep the steps, give the place a vacuum, or even a coat of neutrally coloured emulsion – as long as the other flatowners don't object.

Brighten your property's hallway, maybe sanding the floorboards or installing a neutral carpet and adding extra lighting. If the place is small, keep the doors open when you show people around as it makes the rooms look bigger. In summer open the windows, in winter put the heat up to make the place cosy.

By all means bake bread, grind some coffee beans, make a real fire, put soothing music on, use soft lighting and place fresh flowers around the place when prospective buyers come to view, but it is more important to ensure your home is clean, tidy, aired and uncluttered. Salivating, growling dogs, grumpy teenagers and demanding children can be a real turn off. Don't have a bath or shower before viewers arrive as the bathroom will be steamy and it may look like a condensation problem.

The overall impression should be clean, light and simple, using lots of natural materials. There should be little highly patterned paper and fabric, but the odd splash of bright colour is welcome. The general effect should be calm and comfortable and not fussy. The more floor space there is, the bigger the rooms will look, so consign your clutter to the charity shop.

Tidy up. If you don't mind living in mild squalor, your prospective buyers may think you're not too concerned about looking after the fabric of the building either. Turn on all the side lights, even in the daytime, to brighten things up.

Cover dated or worn sofas and chairs with large throws in a neutral colour and cover carpet stains with neutrally coloured rugs. Paint tiles white with tile paint and regrout if the grout is grubby.

Has the property had an interesting history? The Public Records Office (**www.pro.gov.uk**) and the British Association of Local History (**www.balh.co.uk**) may be able to help you unearth information.

At present, buyers are especially inspired by things like white bathrooms, wooden decking and terracing, large bedrooms with en suite bathrooms, clean, smart kitchens and family rooms with an open-plan feel, recessed halogen lights, stainless steel and nickel taps, highly polished wood floors, granite, slate and limestone surfaces, power showers and plain blinds.

Surveys show that today's buyer is less keen on things like carpets, radiators, formal dining rooms, brass and gold, polished marble, fussy paint finishes, Venetian and festoon blinds, dried and silk flowers, pot pourri, chintz and highly patterned furnishings, saunas and jacuzzis. They are not keen on shoddy DIY 'improvements' or an absence of period features (in a period home that is).

Add coloured plastic bathroom suites, concrete statues in the garden, mock Tudor beams, Artex ceilings, stone cladding, pebble-dash, ceiling mirrors, louvred doors and wall-to-wall twirly carpets, and you can almost guarantee not to sell your home.

Although there are many things you can do to increase your chances of a quick sale, some initiatives could be a complete waste of money. It's seldom worth splashing out on an expensive new kitchen or bathroom, for instance, as there's little guarantee that potential buyers will like your taste or that it will add value to the property.

Still, if your pig-ugly 1970s kitchen really is beyond redemption maybe a cheap flatpack kitchen from a DIY superstore could tip the balance in your favour – but maybe you could get away with just replacing the cabinet and cupboard doors. Simply replacing the door handles could make a world of difference at a cost of under £20. Remember the floor: rip up the dingy old lino and replace it with something bright and cheap. Give tiles a new lease of life with a coat of tile paint or normal paint with tile primer.

Complete redecoration is seldom necessary and may prompt suspicion of you trying to hide hidden faults like damp patches or cracks. Most people would prefer a cheaper home that they can change to their own requirements, and money's better spent sorting out eyesores like damp patches, scuffed paintwork and peeling wallpaper, or sprucing up a particularly gloomy room with a lick of paint in a neutral colour. Cleaning glazed roofs and windows to let in more sunlight can make a huge difference. Faults spell neglect so eradicate leaking gutters, loose door handles and dripping taps.

It's worth replacing windows that have exceeded their lifespan, but make sure they suit the house. Modern double-glazed uPVC ones won't look good in an ancient cottage. Don't consider replacing the roof unless there are structural problems – it's better to negotiate a lower price if needed. Pay attention to the garden. Mow the grass, trim the hedges, weed the flowerbeds. Mature or well-maintained or well-designed and easy-to-maintain gardens all obviously attract buyers but a water feature like a pond may count against the property if the buyer has small children. With Britain's climate, uncovered swimming pools are unlikely to add to the price and may even lower it.

Sorting such problems out before going on to the market also lessens the chances of a potential sale collapsing at the surveying stage. Sometimes the buyer loves a property only to be scared off by an over-cautious surveyor who will point out potential problems, often simply saying that a raft of petty things need further investigation, if only to cover himself. If a survey finds problems you didn't know about, put them right. Don't assume that the next surveyor will miss the problem – he won't.

Have utility and maintenance bills, invoices for work done such as rewiring as well as damp-proofing, timber treatment guarantees and similar paperwork to show potential buyers.

Do not hover behind viewers as they look around, but give them ample chance to inspect the property at their own pace.

Work with your estate agent to ensure the best presentation of your property as possible. Beware using unseasonal photographs on the property particulars. A pretty picture of your home covered in snow displayed in the summer will make buyers assume the property has been languishing unsold since the winter.

PUBLICITY

If your property has some interesting aspect to it – maybe it is unusual architecturally or someone famous has lived in it, for example, it may be worth approaching the local paper or even a national, which may be interested in featuring your home.

PUSHING THE PRICE UP FURTHER

If you're lucky enough to own a property that can generate competition from prospective buyers, there are several sale methods that can help push the price up even further.

SEALED BIDS

You could opt for sealed bids, a non-binding method, reminiscent of the Scottish system, to obtain the best price subject to contract and giving everyone interested a fair chance of purchasing the property. You or your agent invites all interested parties to submit their best offer in writing by a named date, and may ask for references and financial details while stipulating a completion date. The envelopes are opened in the presence of a third party and the best bid wins, although you are not obliged to accept any bid. The best bid is not necessarily the highest. A cash or first-time buyer ready to move quickly may be more attractive than a buyer offering more but still awaiting the sale of their own house.

TELEPHONE AUCTION

Your agent could instead organise a telephone auction where all interested parties have a chance to outbid each other on a certain day and time until the top price is reached. It speeds up the process of weeding out less committed parties. You are not bound by the bids, which are subject to contract.

GAZUMPING

While it is morally wrong to accept the offer of a gazumper – someone who offers more than the price you have already agreed with your buyer – if they are offering a price you would find difficult to turn down, one answer could be to pay the expenses incurred by the first, unsuccessful buyer.

GAZUNDERING

Before the exchange of contracts has taken place the vendor is at risk of gazundering, which is gazumping in reverse, when the buyer threatens to pull out unless the price is reduced. Some lenders offer insurance against this possibility.

SELLING IN SCOTLAND

If you are selling a property in Scotland you will need to appoint a solicitor before selling, who will make sure that your title to the property is in order. He will conduct local authority searches to see whether there are any planned developments that could affect the property.

The solicitor may be able to sell the property for you through its property centre, and the commission is usually around 1 to 1.5 per cent with a small fee for registering the property and the conveyancing charge in addition. If you use an estate agent, the charges will be similar to those in England.

You can negotiate with the first prospective buyer that comes along, but many sellers wait until there are several people expressing a serious interest in the property, at which time the solicitor sets a closing date for offers. You are not obliged to accept any of the offers at the closing date, but prospective buyers are legally required to stick by their offers.

If there is serious interest in your property from more than one prospective buyer, the estate agent or solicitor will typically fix a closing date for offers to be lodged. You are not under any obligation to accept any of the offers.

When you accept an offer your solicitor will adjust points and confirm things with the buyer's solicitor. This is known as 'the missives' and constitutes a legally binding contract.

12 A SECOND HOME

The past decade has seen a dramatic increase in buyers of second homes, whether as a weekend retreat, holiday home and/or long-term investment.

A WEEKEND RETREAT

Such a property should be secure and easy to maintain, so you don't spend your precious leisure time tending the garden or household repairs.

Anything over about three hours' travel time to a weekend retreat is likely to discourage the use of it for that purpose. Bear in mind that the peak time for traffic leaving cities is usually on Friday evenings, and return journeys on Sunday afternoons and evenings can be heavy too. If you plan to let the property on a short-term basis through a holiday cottage rental company, contact several before buying as the criteria for taking properties on can be strict and precise.

A HOLIDAY HOME

Travel times are obviously less important for a property you plan to visit far less frequently, but security and maintenance remain important issues. Again, contact holiday rental agencies before buying if you wish to gain income from the property this way, and bear in mind that it is likely that the agency will want the property to be available just at the times you will want it, such as during the summer.

A HOLIDAY HOME ABROAD

The huge upsurge in British buyers purchasing abroad, principally in France and Spain, ensures there are now many British companies specialising in selling holiday homes abroad. Many advertise in the property sections of national newspapers and there are regular international property exhibitions, as well as magazines dedicated to buying in countries such as France, Spain and Italy.

Property laws abroad of course vary greatly. British legal firms specialising in property purchase abroad are listed at the end of the chapter.

TIMESHARE

About one million Britons now take timeshare holidays. There are
now over 4,700 resorts worldwide in countries as diverse as
Hungary, Senegal and India.

The industry has received plenty of negative publicity concerning
high-pressure selling and dodgy deals, but reputable names like
Marriott, Disney, Airtours, Hilton, Hyatt, Stakis and Four Seasons
now dominate the market.

A 1997 EU Timeshares Directive giving added protection to
purchasers, including a statutory 'cooling off period', has been
taken up by many European states which increases the confidence
of buyers.

The idea of just buying a single unit in one block and being limited
to that block for the rest of your life is now history. You can be more
flexible on the type of unit or time of year, or you can opt for a point
system, a currency to exchange, rather than buy at a specific resort.

A package holiday to Spain costs a family of four typically
£2,000–£2,500. With timeshare you typically pay £10,000 now and,
apart from flights and an annual maintenance charge, you don't
have to pay anything more for sixty years.

To many people, timeshare suggests resorts in Spain or America
but the UK has its own growing market, with over 120 resorts,
double the number 10 years ago.

Timeshare weeks vary greatly in price depending upon the
location, resort, time of year and length of lease. You may be paying
under £5,000 for the least popular weeks and a hefty premium for
school holiday weeks.

Some buyers benefit by buying weeks at a timeshare resort near
their UK home, use its facilities throughout the year, such as a
gym, and then exchange the weeks bought for others abroad.

RENTING A SECOND HOME

Many people dream of owning a cosy country cottage to escape to
at weekends, but the reality can be far from relaxing. Two houses
and gardens to maintain, two sets of bills to pay, security worries
and a traffic-choked motorway to navigate between them. That
idyllic retreat can soon become a burden, with the owner feeling
obliged to visit regularly.

A growing number of people contemplating a second home are
instead choosing to rent instead of buy, and there are loads of
reasons why it makes sense. You can get to know an area well
without having to commit yourself to many months of mortgage
payments.

If you lease a property only from April to September each year, as many rural renters do, you escape the dark, cold, muddy winters but can really get to know what owning a holiday home is like during the sunniest months.

Renting is also an excellent way of testing the water if your long-term dream is to live permanently in the country. Selling your city home and, if you have children, taking them out of the school they are settled in only to find that the move out isn't for you and you want to move back, can be a traumatic experience, especially if house prices have risen more sharply in the city than in the country in the interim. By renting for six months, and staying at weekends and during school holidays, you can see the day-to-day drawbacks but preserve the equity in your city home and precious place at your childrens' over-subscribed school.

Renting a country home is one of the many subjects covered in *Moving to the Country* by Huon Mallalieu which is full of essential information for townies wanting to move to the country. Mallalieu was inspired to write the book after hearing story after story of people who had returned to the city when their rural dream turned sour.

Renting offers unrivalled flexibility. Some renters lease near the coast in the summer for a spot of sailing, and then move to an inland shire for country sports in the winter. The tenancy can be flexible too: an annual renewable tenancy, a longer lease, a short let or a less formal agreement with friends to share the costs.

USEFUL TELEPHONE NUMBERS/ EMAIL ADDRESSES

A HOLIDAY HOME ABROAD

Specialist solicitors: Withers, 020 7936 1000; Russell-Cooke Potter and Chapman, 020 8789 9111; John Howell and Co, 020 7420 0400; Croft Baker and Co, 020 7395 4303; Baily Gibson, 01494 672661; Cornish and Co, 020 8478 3300. The Federation of Overseas Property Developers, Agents and Consultants (F.O.P.D.A.C.), 3rd Floor, 95 Aldwych, London WC2B 4JF; 020 8941 5588, can supply a list of its members.

TIMESHARE

Interval International, 020 8336 9300; RCI, 01536 314445.

APPENDIX A
GLOSSARY OF PROPERTY TERMS

Advance: Mortgage loan.

Adverse credit: A poor credit record.

A.P.R.: Annual percentage rate. Usually shown after the headline rate for a mortgage, the A.P.R. shows the total cost of the loan and should incorporate extras like booking and valuation fees.

Arrangement fee: A fee payable to a mortgage lender for setting up the loan. Normally payable upon completion, it can sometimes be added to the loan.

Assignment: Transfer of ownership to another party of certain kinds of property, for example, a lease or endowment mortgage insurance policy.

A.S.U.: Accident, sickness and unemployment insurance.

Base rate: The Bank of England's rate of interest. Lenders sometimes refer to their standard variable rate as their base rate.

Booking fee: A fee payable to a mortgage lender for securing a particular mortgage offer. Payable on application.

Bridging loan: A short-term loan, usually from a bank, if there is a gap between buying one property and receiving the proceeds of the sale of another and/or when mortgage funds become available.

Buildings insurance: Cover for the structure and fabric of your home.

Buildings survey: A detailed survey of a property.

Buy-to-let mortgage: A loan for buying an investment property. The income that the property can generate from letting is most important, unlike a standard mortgage, where salary is a main factor.

Capital: Your money owned outright. If you buy a property for £100,000 with a £70,000 mortgage, you will need £30,000 of capital to make up the extra. The 'capital' in a repayment mortgage is the amount borrowed and excludes the interest charged on the loan.

Capped rate: A rate of interest on a mortgage with an upper limit but which becomes variable in the event of the lender's standard variable rate falling below that level.

Cashback: A lump sum or percentage of the loan paid on completion as an enticement for the mortgage deal.

C.C.J.: County court judgement, given for non-payment of a debt. If the debt is settled within thirty days of judgement, the C.C.J. will not appear on your credit record. C.C.J.s usually mean high street lenders will decline granting a mortgage, although specialist lenders may do so.

Chain: When more than one property transaction is taking place at the same time and they are linked together. So if A is buying from B, who is buying from C, and so on.

Charge: Any right of interest that freehold or leasehold property may be held, such as a mortgage. Also the term denoting a debit or claim for payment.

Completion: When a property purchase is finalised and you can move in.

Conditions of sale: The detailed terms governing the duties and rights of the purchaser and vendor of a property as laid down in the contract they both sign.

Contents insurance: Cover for the contents of your home rather than the building itself.

Conversion/converted flat: A self-contained flat that was at one time part of a bigger property.

Conveyance: A legal document transferring unregistered land from seller to buyer.

Conveyancing: The legal processes involved in buying or selling a property.

Covenant: A promise in a deed to undertake or abstain from doing specified things.

Credit check/score: A lender's method of finding out how risky it is to take you on as a borrower.

Creditor: Someone owed money, such as the mortgage lender.

Deeds: See *Title deeds*.

Default: Failure to pay a debt, such as a monthly mortgage payment.

Deposit: Money paid to the vendor on exchange of contracts.

Disbursements: The costs added to a solicitor's bill, such as local searches and Land Registry fees.

Discharge fee: The costs charged by a lender to release its charge over your property once you have paid off your loan.

Discounted rate: A variable interest rate that is a certain percentage below the lender's standard variable rate for a set period.

Drawdown facility: The ability to borrow an extra amount through your morgage at a later date.

Early redemption penalty: A lender's charge for repaying the loan before a given date, for example to switch mortgages.

Easement: The legal right of the owner of a property to use the facilities of another person's land, such as a right of way.

Endowment: Life insurance that has an investment element and which therefore can be coupled to a mortgage loan to pay it off at the end of the term.

Equity: The proportion of the property you own outright. It could be the property value less the amount outstanding on the mortgage.

Estate agent: Someone who markets property on the behalf of vendors.

Exchange of contracts (England and Wales only): The point when contracts are swapped to make buyer and seller legally committed to the deal.

Feudal tenure: The system of property ownership in Scotland. The owner of the property is often known as the *feuar* and the property itself may be called the *feu*.

First charge: The legal charge a lender has over your property, so that it is first in the queue for funds available from your property's sale to cover the loan.

First-time buyer: Someone who hasn't owned property before. Lenders and housebuilders especially may offer preferential terms.

Fixed rate: The interest rate on a mortgage is set by the lender for a set period and does not change even if the lender's standard variable rate does.

Flexible mortgage: A mortgage with the facility to make penalty-free, over- and under-payments, drawdowns and other flexible features.

Freehold: Outright ownership of the property and its land.

Full-status mortgage: A home loan where full checks are made on the applicant's income and credit history.

Gazumping: When a purchaser has had their offer accepted but is beaten before contracts are exchanged by another party offering a higher price.

Ground rent: A set sum payable by a leaseholder to the owner of the land on which the property stands.

Guarantor: A person prepared to guarantee your loan, such as a parent, and who would be legally liable for its repayment were you to default.

Homebuy: A housing association scheme offering a loan for a quarter of the cost of the property, with the remainder funded by a mortgage.

Homebuyer's report: A property survey, more extensive than a lender's valuation but more basic than a full structural survey.

Housing association: A non-profit-making registered social landlord which offers ownership and rental schemes.

Independent financial adviser (I.F.A.): An adviser not tied to a particular investment company.

Interest-only mortgage: A loan where you pay interest only, with the full amount loaned payable at the end of the term. An investment vehicle should be in place to cover the loan.

ISA: Individual savings account. Gives the ability to invest in stocks, shares, life assurance and cash tax free, and can be used in repaying an interest-only mortgage.

Land certificate: The document from the Land Registry stating your ownership of a property.

Land Registry: A government department that keeps and amends the registers of all properties in England and Wales with registered titles.

Lease: A written agreement between a landlord and tenant that typically lasts more than seven years, setting out the legal obligations of both.

Leasehold: Ownership of a property for a set amount of time.

Legal charge: Another word for mortgage.

Lender's reference: An endorsement from a lender stating whether you have kept up to date with your mortgage payments.

Lessee: Tenant.

Lessor: Landlord.

Letting: Where a landlord rents out their property to a tenant.

Licensed conveyancer: A person able to handle the legal aspects of property transactions but who is not a qualified lawyer.

Life insurance: A policy payable on death or on a specified date.

Local authority search: A search of local authority records, usually conducted by your solicitor, to confirm the status of the property and reveal possible changes in the locality that could affect the property.

Lock-in period: A specified period after a special mortgage deal has expired where you can only pay off the mortgage if you pay a pre-agreed penalty.

Lock-out agreement: A legal contract initiated by a purchaser requiring the vendor to take the property off the market for a specified period, to prevent gazumping.

L.T.V.: Loan to value. This is the amount of money you are borrowing through a mortgage compared to the value of the property.

M.I.G.: Mortgage indemnity guarantee. This is a one-off insurance premium which may be payable to the lender if you have no or only a small deposit for the home you are buying.

Missives: The Scottish equivalent of exchanging contracts.

Mortgage: Although commonly used to describe a loan granted to buy a property, the term in its correct form is the security you offer your lender in return for the loan, which is usually a legal claim on the property.

Mortgage broker: Adviser or intermediary for finding suitable mortgages for a client.

Mortgagee: Lender of money on the security of a mortgage, such as a building society or bank.

Mortgage term: The amount of time by which you have agreed to pay back your mortgage loan.

Mortgagor: A person borrowing money on a mortgage.

Negative equity: When a mortgage loan is of a higher value than the value of the property.

Non-status mortgage: A mortgage approved without the lender looking into your credit history or income and therefore usually more expensive.

Open market value: The amount a property reaches when there are both a willing purchaser and seller.

Particulars: The descriptions of properties provided by estate agents.

Pension mortgage: An interest-only mortgage where the repayment vehicle is in the form of a personal pension.

Period features: Items in an older home dating back to when it was built, such as a fireplace or ceiling mouldings.

Purpose-built flat: A self-contained flat in a building designed as a complex of flats sharing a common entrance.

Redemption penalty period: A specified period after a special mortgage deal has expired where you can only pay off the mortgage if you pay a pre-agreed penalty.

Relocation agent: A professional property finder for a prospective buyer.

Remortgage: Switching to a new mortgage on your home, usually to release equity or obtain a better rate of interest.

Repayment mortgage: Monthly payments on this loan gradually pay back both interest and capital.

Repayment vehicle: Method of repayment of an interest-only mortgage, such as an investment like an endowment or pension.

Restrictive covenants: Don'ts, that is, restrictions applying to the use of land.

Retention: The withholding of part of a mortgage loan, payable when structural defects on a property are repaired.

R.S.L.: Registered social landlord, that is, a housing association.

Search: See *Local authority search*.

Second mortgage: A further, separate loan on a property in addition to the original mortgage, either with the existing lender or a new one.

Self-build: Where you find the plot, design and build your own home, either yourself or employing others.

Self-certification: Where you state your income to a mortgage lender and it is usually accepted without any or many checks.

Shared ownership: Buying a home in partnership with a housing association, with the intention of increasing your proportion of ownership until it is owned outright by you.

Sitting tenant: A person with a legal right of occupation even if the property is bought by someone else.

Sole occupancy: Where only you and your family reside in the property and there are no paying tenants.

Special-status mortgage: A mortgage approved without the lender looking into your credit history or income and therefore usually more expensive.

Stamp duty: A government tax on the purchase price of a property.

Standard construction: The most common form of building, that is, brick walls with a slate or tiled roof.

Standard variable rate: The basic rate of interest offered by a lender.

Studio flat: A one-room property with attached bathroom and possibly a separate kitchen.

Sub-prime: A borrower with an adverse credit history.

Sum assured: The maximum amount an insurance company will pay out on a policy.

Survey: A professional report on the condition of a property.

Tenancy agreement: A written agreement between landlord and tenant. If it lasts more than seven years it is likely to be called a lease.

Term insurance: Life insurance that will only pay out if you die by the end of the term of the policy.

Title deeds: The legal document proving ownership of a property.

Tracker rate: A mortgage loan that mirrors a base rate such as that of the Bank of England.

Valuation: An inspection on behalf of a lender to establish the value of a property.

Vendor: Someone who is selling a property.

Voluntary purchase: Local authority schemes subsidising the buying of homes by tenants.

APPENDIX B CONTACTS

Ancient Monuments Society, St Ann's Vestry Hall,
2 Church Entry, London EC4V 5HB, 020 7236 3934,
www.ancientmonumentssociety.org.uk

Architects and Surveyors Institute (A.S.I.), 15 St Mary Street,
Chippenham, Wiltshire SN15 3WD, 01249 444505, **www.asi.org.uk**

Architects Registration Board, 8 Weymouth Street, London W1W
5BU, 020 7580 5861, **www.arb.org.uk**

Architectural Association, 34–36 Bedford Square, London WC1B
3ES, 020 7636 0974, **www.archinet.co.uk**

Architecture Foundation, 60 Bastwick Street, London EC1V 3TN,
020 7253 3334, **www.architecturefoundation.org.uk**

Architectural Heritage Fund, Clareville House, 26–27 Oxendon
Street, London SW1Y 4EL, 020 7925 0199, **www.ahfund.org.uk**

Association of British Insurers (A.B.I.), 51 Gresham Street, London
EC2V 7HQ, 020 7600 3333, **www.abi.org.uk**

Association of Building Engineers (A.B.E.), Lutyens House, Billing
Brook Road, Weston Favell, Northampton NN3 8NW, 01604 404121,
www.abe.org.uk

Association of Relocation Agents, PO Box 189, Diss IP22 1NE, 08700
737475, **www.relocationagents.com**

Association of Residential Letting Agents (A.R.L.A.), Maple House,
53–55 Woodside Road, Amersham, Buckinghamshire HP6 6AA,
0845 345 5752, **www.arla.co.uk**

Association of Specialist Underpinning Contractors, 99 West Street,
Farnham, Surrey GU9 7EN, 01252 739143, **www.asuc.org.uk**

Banking and Building Societies Ombudsman, 103 Marsh Wall,
London E14 9SH, 020 7404 9944, **www.obo.org.uk**

British Antique Dealers Association, 20 Rutland Gate, London SW7 1BD, 020 7589 4128, **www.bada.org**

British Association of Removers (B.A.R.), 3 Churchill Court, 58 Station Road, North Harrow, Middlesex HA2 7SA, 020 8861 3331, **www.barmovers.com**

British Holiday and Home Parks Association, Chichester House, 6 Pullman Court, Great Western Road, Gloucester GL1 3ND, 01452 526911, **www.ukparks.com**

British Insurance and Investment Brokers Association (B.I.I.B.A.), B.I.I.B.A. House, 14 Bevis Marks, London EC3A 7NT, 020 7623 9043, **www.biba.org.uk**

British Pest Control Association, Gleneagles House, Vernongate, Derby DE1 1UP, 01332 294288, **www.bpca.org.uk**

British Photovoltaic Association, Davy Avenue, Knowlhill, Milton Keynes MK5 8NG, 01908 442291, **www.pv-uk.org.uk**

British Waterways, Willow Grange, Church Road, Watford, Herts WD17 4QA, 01923 201120, **www.britishwaterways.co.uk**

British Wood Preserving and Damp-proofing Association, 1 Gleneagles House, Vernongate, South Street, Derby DE1 1UP, 01332 225100, **www.bwpda.co.uk**

Building Societies Association, 3 Savile Row, London W1X 1AF, 020 7437 0655, **www.bsa.org.uk**

Cadw: Welsh Historic Monuments, National Assembly for Wales, Cathays Park, Cardiff CF10 3NQ, 02920 500200, **www.cadw.wales.gov.uk**

Centre for Alternative Technology, Machynlleth, Powys SY20 9AZ, 01654 705950, **www.cat.org.uk**

Chartered Institute of Arbitrators, 12 Bloomsbury Square, London WC1A 2LP, 020 7421 7444, **www.arbitrators.org**

Church Commissioners, Redundant Churches Division, 1 Millbank, London SW1P 3JZ, 020 7898 1000, **www.churchcommissioners.org.uk**

Controller of Stamps, Stamp Offices, South West Wing, Bush House, Strand, London WC2B 4QN, 020 7438 6622, **www.inlandrevenue.gov.uk/so**

Council for Energy Efficiency Development, PO Box 12, Haselmere, Surrey GU27 3AH, 01428 654011, **www.insulation.org.uk**

Council for Licensed Conveyancers (C.L.C.), 16 Glebe Road, Chelmsford, Essex CM1 1QG, 01245 349599, **www.conveyancer.org.uk**

Council of Mortgage Lenders (C.M.L.), 3 Savile Row, London W1X 1AF, 020 7440 2255, **www.cml.org.uk**

Council of Registered Gas Installers (CORGI), 1 Elmwood, Chineham Business Park, Crockford Lane, Basingstoke, Hampshire RG24 8WG, 01256 372200, **www.corgi-gas.com**

Data Protection Commissioner, Wycliffe House, Water Lane, Wilmslow, Cheshire SK9 5AF, 01625 545745, **www.dataprotection.gov.uk**

Dry Stone Walling Association of Great Britain, PO Box 8615, Sutton Coldfield, West Midlands B75 7HQ, 0121 378 0493, **www.dswa.org.uk**

Electrical Contractors' Association (E.C.A.), ESCA House, 34 Palace Court, London W2 4HY, 020 7313 4800, **www.eca.co.uk**

Electrical Contractors' Association of Scotland (E.C.A. Scotland), Bush House, Bush Estate, Midlothian EH26 0SB, 0131 445 5577, **www.select.org.uk**

English Heritage, 23 Savile Row, London W1X 1AB, 020 7973 3000, **www.english-heritage.org.uk**

English Historic Towns Forum, PO Box 22, Bristol BS16 1RZ, 0117 975 0459, **www.ehtf.org.uk**

Federation of Master Builders (F.M.B.), 14–15 Great James Street, London WC1N 3DP, 020 7242 7583, **www.fmb.org.uk**

The Financial Services Authority, 25 North Colonnade, London E14 5HS, 020 7676 1000, **www.fsa.gov.uk**

Forestry Commission, 231 Corstorphine Road, Edinburgh EH12 7AT, 0131 334 0303, **www.forestry.gov.uk**

Gas Consumers' Council, Abford House, 15 Wilton Road, London SW1V 1LT, 020 7931 0977

Georgian Group, 6 Fitzroy Square, London W1T 5DX, 020 7529 8920, **www.georgiangroup.org.uk**

Heating and Ventilating Contractors Association (H.V.C.A.), 34 Palace Court, London W2 4JG, 020 7229 2488, **www.hvca.org.uk**

Heritage Lottery Fund and National Heritage Memorial Fund, 7 Holbein Place, London SW1W 8NR, 020 7591 6042, **www.hlf.org**

Historic Houses Association, 2 Chester Street, London SW1X 7BB, 020 7259 5688, **www.hha.org.uk**

Housing Corporation, 149 Tottenham Court Road, London W1P 0BN, 020 7393 2000, **www.housingcorp.gov.uk**

Housing Division, National Assembly for Wales, Cardiff Bay, Cardiff CF99 1NA, 02920 825111, **www.wales.gov.uk**

Independent Financial Advice Bureau, 549 Green Lanes, London N8 0RQ, 020 8348 4466

Independent Financial Advice Promotion, 28 Greville Street, London EC1N 8SU, 0117 971 1177, **www.ifap.org.uk**

Inland Revenue, helpline 0845 603 0135, **www.inlandrevenue.gov.uk**

Institute of Plumbing, 64 Station Lane, Hornchurch, Essex RM12 6NB, 01708 472791, **www.plumbers.org.uk**

Insurance Ombudsman Bureau, South Quay, Plaza Two, 183 Marsh Wall, London E14 9SR, 08456 006666, **www.theiob.org.uk**

Land Registry, 32 Lincoln's Inn Fields, London WC2A 3PH, 020 7917 8888, **www.landreg.gov.uk**

Lands Tribunal for Scotland, 1 Grosvenor Crescent, Edinburgh EH12 5ER, 0131 225 7996, **www.edinburgh.gov.uk**

Lapada, 535 King's Road, London SW10 0SZ, 020 7823 3511, **www.lapada.co.uk**

Law Commission, 37–38 John Street, Theobald's Road, London WC1N 2BQ, 020 7435 1220, **www.lawcom.gov.uk**

Law Society, 113 Chancery Lane, London WC2A 1PL, 020 7242 1222; public enquiry line 0870 606 6575 **www.lawsociety.org.uk**

Law Society of Northern Ireland, 98 Victoria Street, Belfast BT1 3JZ, 02890 231614, **www.lawsoc-ni.org**

Law Society of Scotland, 26 Drumsheugh Gardens, Edinburgh EH3 7YR, 0131 226 7411, **www.lawscot.org.uk**

Leasehold Enfranchisement Advisory Service, 6–8 Maddox Street, London W1R 9PN, 020 7493 3116, **www.lease-advice.org**

Legal Services Ombudsman, 22 Oxford Court, Oxford Street, Manchester M2 3WQ, 0161 236 9532, **www.olso.org**

Mediation UK, Alexander House, Telephone Avenue, Bristol BS1 4BS, 0117 904 6661, **www.mediation.org.uk**

National Approval Council for Security Systems (N.A.C.O.S.S.), Queensgate House, 14 Cookham Road, Maidenhead, Berkshire SL6 8AJ, 01628 37512, **www.nacoss.org.uk**

National Approved Letting Scheme (Nals), Warwick Corner, 42 Warwick Road, Kenilworth CV8 1HE, 01926 866633, **www.nalscheme.co.uk**

National Association of Chimney Sweeps, Unit 15 Emerald Way, Stone Business Park, Stone, Staffordshire ST15 0SR, 01785 811732, **www.chimneyworks.co.uk**

National Association of Estate Agents (N.A.E.A.), Arbon House, 21 Jury Street, Warwick CV34 4EH, 01926 496800, **www.naea.co.uk**

National Association of Plumbing, Heating and Mechanical Service Contractors (N.A.P.H.M.S.C.), Ensign House, Ensign Business Centre, Westwood Way, Coventry CV4 8JA, 01203 470626

National Federation of Builders, Bridge Court, Bridge Street, Long Eaton, Nottingham NG10 4QQ, 0115 9461922, **www.builders.org.uk**

National Guild of Approved Removers and Storers, 3 High Street, Chesham, Buckinghamshire HP5 1BG, 01494 792279, **www.ngrs.org.uk**

National House Building Council (N.H.B.C.), Buildmark House, Chiltern Avenue, Amersham, Buckinghamshire HP6 5AP, 01494 735363, **www.nhbc.co.uk**

National Housing Federation, 175 Gray's Inn Road, London WC1X 8UP, 020 7278 6571, **www.housing.org.uk**

National Inspection Council for Electrical Installation Contracting (N.I.C.E.I.C.), Vintage House, 37 Albert Embankment, London SE1 7UJ, 020 7564 2323, **www.niceic.org.uk**

National Monuments Record Centre, Kemble Drive, Swindon SN2 2GZ, 01793 414600, **www.english-heritage.org.uk**

National Park Homes Council, Catherine House, Victoria Road, Aldershot, Hampshire GU11 1SS, 01252 318251, **www.theparkhome.net**

National Society of Master Thatchers, 20 The Laurels, Tetsworth, Thame, Oxfordshire OX9 7BH, 01844 281568, **www.nsmt.co.uk**

National Solicitors' Network, 156 Cromwell Road, London SW7 4EF, 020 7244 6422, **www.solicitorsnetwork.co.uk**

National Trust, 36 Queen Anne's Gate, London SW1H 9AS, 0870 609 5380, **www.nationaltrust.org.uk**

New Homes Marketing Board (N.H.M.B.), 82 New Cavendish Street, London W1M 8AD, 020 7580 5588, **www.hbf.co.uk**

Northern Ireland Co-ownership Housing Association, 02890 327276, **www.co-ownership.org**

Northern Ireland Housing Executive, Housing Centre, 2 Adelaide Street, Belfast, 02890 240588, **www.nihe.gov.uk**

Office for the Supervision of Solicitors, Victoria Court, 8 Dormer Place, Leamington Spa, Warwickshire CV32 5AE, 01926 820082

Office of Gas and Electricity Markets (O.F.G.E.M.), 9 Millbank, London SW1P 3GE, 020 7901 7000/0800 887777, **www.ofgem.gov.uk**

Office of Water Services (O.F.W.A.T.), 7 Hill Street, Birmingham B5 4UA, 0121 625 1300, **www.ofwat.gov.uk**

Ombudsman for Estate Agents, 4 Bridge Street, Salisbury, Wiltshire SP1 2LX, 01722 332296/333306, **www.oea.co.uk**

Organisation for Timeshare in Europe (O.T.E.), 020 7821 8845, **www.ote-info.com**

Rail Property, B.R.B. (Residuary), Whittles House, 14 Pentonville Road, London N1 9RP, 020 7904 5100, **www.brbr.gov.uk**

Registry Trust, 173–175 Cleveland Street, London W1P 5PE

Residential Boat Owners' Association, PO Box 518, Rickmansworth WD3 1WJ, **www.rboa.co.uk**

Royal Commission on Ancient and Historic Monuments of Scotland, John Sinclair House, 16 Bernard Terrace, Edinburgh EH8 9NX, 0131 662 1456, **www.rcahms.gov.uk**

Royal Commission on Ancient and Historic Monuments of Wales, Plas Crug, Aberystwyth, Ceredigion, Wales SY23 1NJ, 01907 621200, **www.rcahmw.org.uk**

Royal Incorporation of Architects in Scotland, 15 Rutland Square, Edinburgh EH1 2BE, 0131 229 7205, **www.rias.org.uk**

Royal Institute of British Architects (R.I.B.A.), 66 Portland Place, London W1N 4AD, 020 7580 5533/020 7307 3700, **www.architecture.com**

Royal Institution of Chartered Surveyors (R.I.C.S.), 12 Great George Street, London SW1P 3AD, 020 7222 7000, **www.rics.org.uk**

Royal Institution of Chartered Surveyors in Scotland, 9 Manor Place, Edinburgh EH3 7DN, 0131 225 7078, **www.rics-scotland.org.uk**

Royal Society of Architects in Wales, 75a Llandennis Road, Rhydypennau, Cardiff CF2 6EE, 02920 874753, **www.architecture.com**

Royal Society of Ulster Architects, 2 Mount Charles, Belfast BT7 1NZ, 01232 323760, **www.rsua.org.uk**

The Royal Town Planning Institute, 41 Botolph Lane, London EC3R 8DL, 020 7929 9494, **www.rtpi.org.uk**

SAVE Britain's Heritage, 70 Cowcross Street, London EC1M 6EJ, 020 7253 3500, **www.savebritainsheritage.org**

Scottish Building Employers' Federation, Carron Grange, Carron Grange Avenue, Stenhousemuir FK5 3BQ, 01324 555550

Scottish Civic Trust, 42 Miller Street, Glasgow G1 1DT, 0141 221 1466, **www.scotnet.co.uk/sct**

Scottish Conveyancing and Executry Services Board, 1 John's Place, Leith, Edinburgh EH6 7EL, 0131 555 6525, **www.scesb.co.uk**

Scottish Federation of Housing Associations, 38 York Place, Edinburgh EH1 3HU, 0131 556 5777, **www.sfha.co.uk**

Self-Build Advisory Service, 0131 524 8500

Shelter, 88 Old Street, London EC1V 9HU, **www.shelter.org.uk**

Small Landlord's Association, 78 Tachbrook Street, London SW1 2NA, 0870 241 0471, **www.landlords.org.uk**

Society for the Protection of Ancient Buildings (S.P.A.B.), 37 Spital Square, London E1 6DY, 020 7377 1644, **www.spab.org.uk**

Society of Fine Art Auctioneers, London Road, Send, Woking, Surrey GU23 7LN, 01483 225891, **www.sofaa.org**

Society of Licensed Conveyancers, 55 Church Road, Croydon CR9 1PF, 020 8681 1001, **www.conveyancers.org.uk**

Solicitors Property Group, 30 Station Road, Cuffley, Hertfordshire EN6 4HE, 01707 873126, **www.solicitorspropertygroup.co.uk**

Subsidence Claims Advisory Bureau, Charter House, 43 St Leonards Road, Bexhill-on-Sea, East Sussex TN40 1JA, 01424 733727, **www.bureauinsure.co.uk**

Thatching Advisory Services, Faircross Offices, Stratfield Saye, Reading, Berkshire RG7 2BT, 01256 880828, **www.thatchingadvisoryservices.co.uk**

Timber and Brick Homes Information Council, Gable House, 40 High Street, Rickmansworth, Hertfordshire WD3 1ES

Twentieth Century Society, 70 Cowcross Street, London EC1M 6EJ, 020 7250 3857, **www.c20society.demon.co.uk**

Ulster Architectural Heritage Society, 66 Donegall Pass, Belfast BT7 1BU, 02890 550213, **www.uahs.co.uk**

Vernacular Architecture Group, 01245 361408, **www.worthingtonm.freeserve.co.uk/vag/**

Victorian Society, 1 Priory Gardens, Bedford Park, London W4 1TT, 020 8994 1019, **www.victorian-society.org.uk**

Yacht Brokers, Designers and Surveyors Association, Wheel House, Petersfield Road, Whitehill, Borden, Hampshire GU35 9BU, 01420 473862, **www.ybdsa.co.uk**

Zurich Municipal, Gemini Court, 7 Thomas More Street, London E1 9YR, 020 7265 1033, **www.zurichmunicipal.com**

INDEX